Inspired Words

Inspired Words

—— Devotions for Readers ——

Nancy Knol
and
Brian Karsten

RESOURCE *Publications* · Eugene, Oregon

INSPIRED WORDS
Devotions for Readers

Resource Publications
An Imprint of Wipf and Stock Publishers
199 W. 8th Ave., Suite 3
Eugene, OR 97401

www.wipfandstock.com

PAPERBACK ISBN: 978-1-7252-7788-5
HARDCOVER ISBN: 978-1-7252-7787-8
EBOOK ISBN: 978-1-7252-7789-2

03/03/21

Author is represented by the literary agency of Credo Communications, LLC, Grand Rapids, Michigan, credocommunications.net.

All Scripture quotations, unless otherwise indicated, are taken from the Holy Bible, New International Version®, NIV®. Copyright ©1973, 1978, 1984, 2011 by Biblica, Inc.® Used by permission of Zondervan. All rights reserved worldwide. www.zondervan.com The "NIV" and "New International Version" are trademarks registered in the United States Patent and Trademark Office by Biblica, Inc.®

"All Summer In A Day" Reprinted by permission of Don Congdon Associates, Inc. © 1954, renewed 1982 by Ray Bradbury.

By the Waters of Babylon by Stephen Vincent Benet. Copyright © 1937 by Stephen Vincent Benet, Copyright renewed © 1965 by Thomas C. Benet, Stephanie Mahin and Rachel B. Lewis. Used by permission of Brandt & Hochman Literary Agents, Inc. All rights reserved.

Excerpts from "The Hollow Men" from COLLECTED POEMS 1909-1962 by T.S. Eliot. Copyright © 1925 Houghton Mifflin Harcourt Publishing Company, renewed 1953 by Thomas Stearns Eliot. Reprinted by permission of Houghton Mifflin Harcourt Publishing Company. All rights reserved.

To John, who cheers me on with steadfast certainty
—Nancy

To Ellory, who loves books now and, I hope, forever
—Brian

Contents

Preface | xv

Beauty

Looking Again: "Nature" by Ralph Waldo Emerson,
Psalm 98:7-8a (Knol) | 3

This Amazing Day: "i thank You God for most this amazing"
by e.e. cummings, Psalm 19:1-4 (Karsten) | 5

Truth

We Wear the Mask: "We Wear the Mask" by Paul Laurence
Dunbar, Jeremiah 12:3 (Knol) | 9

The Naked Truth: *The Crucible* by Arthur Miller, Luke 8:17
(Knol) | 12

If the Answer Matters, You've Got Your Answer: *The Things
They Carried* by Tim O'Brien, John 16:13 (Karsten) | 15

You Shall be Free Indeed: *The Orphan Master's Son*
by Adam Johnson, John 8:31-32 (Knol) | 17

The Truth About Gold: "Nothing Gold Can Stay"
by Robert Frost, Jeremiah 16:33 (Knol) | 19

Sin and Forgiveness

Who? Me?: "The Possibility of Evil" by Shirley Jackson,
Ephesians 4:32 (Knol) | 23

Selling One's Soul: "The Devil and Tom Walker" by Washington Irving, Matthew 16:26 (Knol) | 26

That Dirty Word: "The Portable Phonograph" by Walter Van Tilburg Clark, Romans 7:19 (Knol) | 28

Less is More: *Perelandra* by C.S. Lewis, Proverbs 25:16 (Knol) | 31

Gracefully Far and Deep: *In the Lake of the Woods* by Tim O'Brien, James 5:16 (Karsten) | 33

Rotting Bones: *A Separate Peace* by John Knowles, Proverbs 14:30 (Knol) | 35

Remember: *The Kite Runner* by Khaled Hosseini, I Corinthians 11:24-25 (Knol) | 37

Restraint: "Sinners in the Hands of an Angry God" by Jonathan Edwards, Romans 7:21, 23-24 (Knol) | 40

Discernment

Taking Note: "The Red Wheelbarrow" by William Carlos Williams, Matthew 6:28-29 (Knol) | 45

Brain and Heart Hacking: "By the Waters of Babylon" by Stephen Vincent Benet, Proverbs 19:2 (Knol) | 47

Definitely Not Safe: *The Giver* by Lois Lowry, Joshua 24:15 (Karsten) | 49

The Eye That Blinks: *The Chosen* by Chaim Potok, Jeremiah 1:5 (Knol) | 52

Mortal Stakes: "Two Tramps in Mudtime" by Robert Frost, Colossians 3:23 (Knol) | 54

Lines and Circles: *The House on Mango Street* by Sandra Cisneros, Philippians 2:4-5a (Knol) | 56

Yearning

Holy: "Parker's Back" by Flannery O'Connor,
II Corinthians 4:6 (Knol) | 61

Practicing Resurrection: *The Things They Carried*
by Tim O'Brien, I Corinthians 15:55 (Knol) | 63

Heart's Desire: "All Summer in a Day" by Ray Bradbury,
Revelation 21:5 (Knol) | 66

Wisdom

What God Is: *Cat's Cradle* by Kurt Vonnegut, Mark 10:15
(Karsten) | 71

Time Optimists: *A Man Called Ove* by Fredrik Backman,
Psalm 90:12 (Knol) | 73

Small, Good Things: *The Screwtape Letters* by C.S. Lewis,
Psalm 16:11 (Knol) | 75

Greater Complexities: *Things Fall Apart* by Chinua Achebe,
Philippians 4:6-7 (Karsten) | 77

Who's Boss Here?: *Lord of the Flies* by William Golding,
Matthew 10:32-33 (Karsten) | 79

Finding Your Voice: *Their Eyes Were Watching God* by Zora
Neale Hurston, several Proverbs verses (Knol) | 81

Which Way to Jump or Fall: *Fahrenheit 451* by Ray Bradbury,
I Thessalonians 5:19-22 (Karsten) | 84

Going Further into the Matter: *Out of the Silent Planet*
by C.S. Lewis, Matthew 13:10-13 (Karsten) | 86

Purpose

The Big Question: *The Great Gatsby* by F. Scott Fitzgerald, Proverbs 26:15 (Knol) | 91

Fault: *Brave New World* by Aldous Huxley, Ephesians 1:18-19 (Karsten) | 93

Lighting Little Fires Everywhere: *Little Fires Everywhere* by Celeste Ng, Isaiah 6:8 (Knol) | 95

Saying Equals Doing: "Story of Your Life" by Ted Chiang, James 5:13-18 (Karsten) | 98

To Wear an Identity: *Ender's Game* by Orson Scott Card, James 2:18 (Karsten) | 101

Folks: *To Kill a Mockingbird* by Harper Lee, Romans 12:15 (Knol) | 104

Winners and Losers: *Maus II: A Survivor's Tale: And Here My Troubles Began* by Art Spiegelman, Matthew 19:30 (Karsten) | 106

Dangerous Folly: *Macbeth* by William Shakespeare, Galatians 6:9 (Karsten) | 109

Losing Heart: *The Narrative of Frederick Douglass* by Frederick Douglass, and *Walden* by Henry David Thoreau, II Corinthians 4:16-17 (Knol) | 111

Filled with Straw: "The Hollow Men" by T.S. Eliot, Romans 12:2 (Karsten) | 114

Serving or Selfishness: "Sonnet 19" by John Milton, Matthew 23:11-13 (Karsten) | 116

Suffering

Monster: *Frankenstein* by Mary Shelley, Romans 7:24
(Knol) | 121

Meaningless: *Slaughterhouse Five* by Kurt Vonnegut,
I Peter 3:15 (Karsten) | 123

Part of God's Plan: *Testament of Youth* by Vera Brittain,
Romans 12:15 (Karsten) | 126

Standard Equipment: *A Farewell to Arms* by Ernest
Hemingway, Psalm 61:2 (Knol) | 128

Love

Religion or Relationship?: *The Great Divorce* by C.S. Lewis,
John 3:16 (Knol) | 133

More than Conquerors: "Invictus" by William Ernest Henley,
Romans 8:37 (Knol) | 135

How She's Treated: *Pygmalion* by George Bernard Shaw,
Matthew 25:40 (Karsten) | 137

Not Enough: *The Grapes of Wrath* by John Steinbeck,
John 14:6a (Knol) | 140

I Should Much Rather Have. . . : *The Chosen* by Chaim Potok,
Proverbs 4:23 (Knol) | 142

What Love Looks Like: *A Farewell to Arms* by Ernest
Hemingway, I John 4:19 (Knol) | 144

Faithfulness

Best-Laid Schemes: "To a Mouse" by Robert Burns,
Jeremiah 29:11 (Karsten) | 149

Mystery: *The Absolutely True Diary of a Part-Time Indian*
by Sherman Alexie, I Corinthians 2:1-5 (Karsten) | 151

Faith: "The River" by Flannery O'Connor, Hebrews 11:1
(Knol) | 154

So It Goes: *Slaughterhouse Five* by Kurt Vonnegut,
Isaiah 46:9-10 (Karsten) | 156

Principles and Belief: *Heart of Darkness* by Joseph Conrad,
James 2:17-18 (Karsten) | 159

Crooked Little Heart: *Crooked Little Heart* by Anne Lamott,
II Corinthians 4:7 (Knol) | 161

Tested: *Silence* by Shūsaku Endō, II Corinthians 4:11
(Knol) | 163

Bibliography | 165

Preface

Joyce Carol Oates once said, "Reading is the sole means by which we slip, involuntarily, often helplessly, into another's skin, another's voice, another's soul."[1] I suspect that for all readers, there is at least one piece of fiction out there that they remember fondly, even years later, because somehow that story shaped their perspective or softened their heart. I remember reading aloud one of the chapters of *To Kill a Mockingbird* to my ninth grade English class several years ago. It was the chapter where Scout is trying to tell Atticus and the sheriff about the attack and about being rescued by *someone*. . . and as she struggles to recount everything, she looks at a man leaning against the wall behind the door. She thinks she doesn't know him, but then "his lips parted into a timid smile, and our neighbor's image blurred with my sudden tears. 'Hey Boo,' I said." One of my students, a delightfully expressive and eager girl who had fallen in love with this book, jumped up from her seat at that moment. "I knew it!" she proclaimed to a shocked but smiling sea of faces, "I just *knew* it would be Boo who saved them!" She sat down, a little embarrassed, but I could have kissed her. And now, years later, I'd like to think she remembers that moment—how she got completely swallowed up into the *story*, and how she was, consciously or not, celebrating the heroic compassion of someone who had lived in the shadows for most of his lonely life.

The stories and poems we have selected for this book have each had an impact on our understanding of the world. We have identified with a character or a moment of pain or joy and have held it close. As professing Christians, we have decided to explore these passages and place them in the light of scripture, which hopefully broadens rather than narrows our understanding of these universal truths. What we believe makes this book valuable

1. Shilling and Fuller, *Dictionary of Quotations in Communications*, 193.

(and perhaps somewhat unusual) as a devotional is its approach of pondering rather than moralizing. Who knows? The reader may find a moment of new awareness about how and where they fit into this world full of challenges and wonders and discover that God is in the thick of it. We are not alone. We belong.

Beauty

Looking Again

To speak truly, few adult persons can see nature. . . At least
they have a very superficial seeing. The sun illuminates on
the eye of the man, but shines into the eye and the heart
of the child.[1]

—RALPH WALDO EMERSON, "NATURE"

One of the sad consequences of growing up is that we lose the
wonder of childhood. I mean "wonder" both in the sense of cu-
riosity *and* of awe. What makes this happen? My students have
speculated that it has to do with things being less new—a rainbow
is beautiful, but we've seen it before. Others think that we just get
too busy to take the time to step out into the world with no other
purpose than discovering it. And some say that adults prompt our
first discoveries but then quit doing it when we get more indepen-
dent about all kinds of things.

Whatever the cause, it is a loss. I remember taking a long
walk with my grandson Wendell when he was three years old.
We went to a park and just wandered through the trees. It was
autumn. Wendell picked up an acorn and brought it to me. I
told him about how an acorn could make a big oak tree if it was
planted in the ground. I picked up the brown "top" of the acorn
to show him how it fit onto what he had found. He began to laugh
and laugh. "What's so funny?" I asked. He began to take the top
off and return it several times. "Hat on, hat off, hat on, hat off," he
kept repeating. I had to laugh too.

Last summer Wendell and I were sitting on our front porch
when a summer storm burst forth. A brief period of hard rain filled
the gullies along the road to overflowing, and then sun. We stepped
outside in our bare feet and splashed in the puddles, and when it

1. Emerson, "Nature," *Nature, Addresses, and Lectures,* 14.

began to rain again, we grabbed umbrellas and walked down the street together. "Nana," he observed, "that one dark cloud is like a great big sponge that God keeps squeezing."

A few adults still remember to stop and wonder. After a big snowfall a few years ago, one friend wrote to me: "The snow is so beautiful this morning where I live. It's the fluffy kind, where, when you put your foot down, it looks like your foot exhaled, leaving a footprint twice its size." And during a particularly lovely spring one year, another friend wrote, "The apple tree in our yard is in full pink wardrobe. . . God's feminine side. God in the pastels, God in the gentler places. . . I need to explore that more."

As Christians, we have been called not only to take care of God's beautiful world but also to delight in it. It is indeed admirable to be vigilant about ecological concerns because it means we are preserving our own welfare and the state of the planet. But it is even better to delight in it and thank God for creating with the heart of a child.

> Let the sea resound, and everything in it, the world, and all who live in it. Let the rivers clap their hands, let the mountains sing together for joy, let them sing before the Lord. (Psalm 98:7–9a, NIV)

This Amazing Day

how should tasting touching hearing seeing
breathing any—lifted from the no
of all nothing—human merely being
doubt unimaginable You?[1]

—E.E. CUMMINGS, "I THANK YOU GOD FOR MOST
THIS AMAZING"

"It's a beautiful day, and I thank God for the weather. It's a beautiful day, and I'm living it for my Lord." These words, sung (or often yelled) enthusiastically by Sunday school students for generations, are simple yet profound. It *is* a beautiful day. And God is to be thanked.

Maybe there's a hummingbird buzzing its wings outside your window as it sips from a newly bloomed flower, or morning dew reflecting the early morning sunshine, or a cool breeze giving relief on a hot, humid day. Or possibly the trees are turning in early autumn and wooded areas are a kaleidoscope of reds, oranges, yellows, and browns. Or there could be a fresh, pure fall of snow blanketing the streets, trees, and homes in your neighborhood, making the world feel fresh. (And offering the possibility of a no-school snow day?)

Too often, however, as we work or study or find other ways to keep ourselves busy, we don't always take note. Regardless of the season, how often do we thank God for the weather? Those Sunday school students should serve as a reminder of something we too often take for granted.

Perhaps e.e. cummings's words could be your prayer today:

---

1. cummings, "i thank You God for most this amazing," *Xaipe*, 70.

i thank you God for most this amazing
day: for the leaping greenly spirits of trees
and a blue true dream of sky; and for everything
which is natural which is infinite which is yes

(i who have died am alive again today,
and this is the sun's birthday; this is the birth
day of life and of love and wings: and of the gay
great happening illimitably earth)

how should tasting touching hearing seeing
breathing any—lifted from the no
of all nothing—human merely being
doubt unimaginable You?

(now the ears of my ears awake and
now the eyes of my eyes are opened)[2]

"The heavens declare the glory of God; the skies proclaim
the work of his hands. Day after day they pour forth
speech; night after night they reveal knowledge. They
have no speech, they use no words; no sound is heard
from them. Yet their voice goes out into all the earth, their
words to the ends of the world." (Psalm 19:1–4, NIV)

---

2. cummings, "i thank You God for most this amazing," *Xaipe*, 70.

Truth

We Wear the Mask

We wear the mask that grins and lies,
It hides our cheeks and shades our eyes
This debt we pay to human guile;
With torn and bleeding hearts we smile,
And mouth with myriad subtleties.

Why should the world be over-wise,
In counting all our tears and sighs?
Nay, let them only see us, while
We wear the mask.

We smile, but, O great Christ, our cries
To thee from tortured souls arise.
We sing, but oh the clay is vile
Beneath our feet, and long the mile;
But let the world dream otherwise,
We wear the mask.[1]

—PAUL LAURENCE DUNBAR, "WE WEAR THE MASK"

There are many people who love to wear masks. Halloween is their big opportunity to disguise themselves as someone else. There is something exciting and powerful about being able to do that. Perhaps you have read R.J. Palacio's popular book *Wonder*, where fifth grader Augie finds safety and solace and even a sense of normalcy by wearing a spaceman helmet that his sister's friend gives him.

---

1. Dunbar, *The Complete Poems of Paul Laurence Dunbar*, 71.

Because Augie's face is severely disfigured, this "mask" gives him the freedom to be like any other kid.

The poet Paul Laurence Dunbar is also celebrating what a mask can offer us. In his case, however, the mask is not an actual mask one puts on but a defense mechanism, an expression which cloaks what we are actually feeling. "It hides our cheeks and shades our eyes." These two parts of the human face are the most revealing in regard to what we are feeling on the inside. Think about it. A blush on the cheeks reveals embarrassment or perhaps excitement. And the eyes, as the saying goes, are the "mirrors to the soul," which means that when you look into a person's eyes you have a pretty good idea what they are made of.

When I taught middle school, our principal instructed all of the elementary and middle school teachers on the first day of staff meetings to be sure to check the files in the main office regarding the students under our care. This was to ensure our awareness of any potential learning, health, or social issues. Whenever I took out the files of my homeroom students, I paused to look at the outside of each folder. Every year when school pictures were taken, the office was given a tiny picture of each student. The secretary then taped them in a row to the outside of each individual file folder. I taught eighth grade, so there were pictures from kindergarten all the way to seventh grade staring up at me. It fascinated me. What was most compelling, and a little sad, was the fact that I could actually see the progression of attitude toward beginning another school year in each face (some more pronounced than others, of course). Kindergarteners all looked either full of excitement or decidedly terrified—most often a bit of a mix of the two. By the time my eyes scanned through to fifth grade, which education experts claim is the most telling year in regard to a student's awareness of how they stand socially and intellectually compared to their peers, it was fairly easy to tell which students found school a pleasant experience and which definitely found it a challenge—or even a drudgery.

If you have people in your life who refuse to let you wear a mask, be grateful. Self-protection is an understandable defense, but self-revelation is what we all desire more than almost anything else. When you have found that friend who loves you "warts and all" and helps you laugh at your weaknesses while celebrating your strengths, you have found one of the most precious gifts God offers. When your parents see through your elaborate deceptions, try to be glad despite the consequences. Someone knows the real you and cares enough to make you accountable. If you are able to pray honestly to God at the end of the day, confessing your sins without trying to excuse yourself and seeking his help in facing the challenges of tomorrow, you are building a real relationship—not going through the motions, not putting on a kind of mask. "We smile, but O great Christ / Our cries to thee from tortured souls arise." That naked honesty can make all the difference between who you pretend to be and who you really are. God is in the business of the latter.

> Yet you know me, O Lord; you see me and test my thoughts about you. (Jeremiah 12:3, NIV)

The Naked Truth

Now Hell and Heaven grapple on our backs, and all our old
pretense is ripped away—make your peace! Peace. It is a
providence, and no great change; we are only what we always were, but naked now. Aye, naked! And the wind, God's
icy wind will blow![1]

—ARTHUR MILLER, *THE CRUCIBLE*

The Crucible is Arthur Miller's heartbreaking, passionate play
condemning two terrible moments of deception in American
history: the 1692 Salem Witch Trials, which is the event the story
centers around, and the 1955 Joseph McCarthy hearings. The
parallels are unnerving. Miller himself said later that "the main
point of the McCarthy hearings, precisely as in seventeenth century Salem, was that the accused make public confession while
damning their friends."[2]

In this scene, John Proctor sees that his world has gone mad
with lies—so much so that his own wife, a sincere and godly woman, has been arrested for witchcraft. He is urging Mary, the young
woman who works for the Proctors and knows the truth about
the lying Abigail, to expose Abigail so that the innocent victims of
her false accusations can go free. Mary is terrified at the prospect;
Abigail has promised "a pointy reckoning that will shudder you"
to anyone who speaks the truth. But in a Shakespeare-like speech,
John seizes Mary by the shoulders and tells her that she must make
her peace with God and proclaim that truth.

Nakedness is often used in literature to symbolically return
the reader to the innocence of Eden, where Adam and Eve "were
both naked and felt no shame." Perhaps one of the best examples

1. Miller, *The Crucible*, 76.
2. Ibid., x.

of nakedness as a symbol of peeling off layers of lies and treachery can be found in Shakespeare's *King Lear*, where Lear, in a moment of what appears to be madness, goes out into a storm naked. The reader soon senses that the king has actually come, finally, to his senses.

Good people like to see lies exposed and the truth prevail. In the June 2017 issue of *National Geographic*, Claudia Kalb made her own list of some of the biggest lies of the last century. Perhaps the most notorious political lie, she claims, was the Nixon Watergate scandal, where Nixon said, "I am not a crook." But on August 9, 1974, his words, clearly a blatant lie, forced him to resign to avoid impeachment. In the world of sports, Kalb chose the 1919 White Sox fiasco, where the team accepted a bribe to throw the World Series. There are lies of identity—Anna Anderson claiming to be the lost Anastasia, daughter of the czar of Russia and only survivor of the execution of her family. And there are lies of finance—certainly Charles Ponzi deserves top billing here. His very name has become synonymous with swindler. Meanwhile, the entertainment world also has some impressive whoopers—in 1938 Orson Welles terrified many listeners as they heard his *War of the Worlds* broadcast and believed that the world was being invaded by aliens. In the field of science, Charles Dawson and Arthur Woodward made a clever fabrication of a skull in 1912 that they claimed proved that humans were half-man and half-ape.[3]

Yes, we like to see truth prevail and lies condemned—at least, when it comes to the lies of *others*. But when it comes to our own moments of truth, we are less eager, are we not? How many times have you been willing to compromise almost *anything* in order to prevent the truth of something foolish or ugly or cruel you have done being identified and addressed with the cold, hard light of truth?

Strangely, the book of Ecclesiastes, a very dark and almost despairing book, ends with what the author seems to suggest is a reason to feel hopeful about life. He says that "God will bring every deed into judgment including every hidden thing, whether it is

3. Kalb, "These Are History's Most Notorious Liars."

good or evil." It is lovely to think that good things—quiet deeds of sacrifice and honor and love—will be given acknowledgment, but it is terrifying to think of "every hidden thing" being brought into view for all the world to see.

Unless you are a lover of truth. And a lover of justice. And a lover of forgiveness. Why should we love truth? Because we can only trust what is true—everything that is a lie leads us in hell's direction and destroys relationships. Why should we love justice? Because life needs to be fair. The scales need to be balanced to make us feel that all is right with the world. And why should we love forgiveness? Because once our ugly secrets have been revealed, the blood of the lamb goes from a "pointy reckoning" to "cleansing us of all unrighteousness." Truth strips us naked. The lie of the serpent in the garden may have made Adam and Eve run for cover—literally. But the truth will set us free.

> For there is nothing hidden that will not be disclosed, and nothing concealed that will not be known or brought out into the open. (Luke 8:17, NIV)

If the Answer Matters,
You've Got Your Answer

> You can tell a true war story by the questions you ask. Somebody tells a story, let's say, and afterwards you ask, "Is it true?" and if the answer matters, you've got your answer.[1]

—TIM O'BRIEN, *THE THINGS THEY CARRIED*

At church last Sunday, our pastor was preaching on the story of the flood. Immediately, it got me thinking of author Tim O'Brien. In his Vietnam War novel *The Things They Carried*, O'Brien leaves his readers wondering how much of his story is true. O'Brien did serve in Vietnam—that is true. O'Brien writes the novel as himself, a writer reflecting on his time in Vietnam. And the characters in his novel, who he writes as real people in real situations, feel true as well, but they aren't. In one particularly impactful story, O'Brien talks about a trip he took to Vietnam with his daughter, decades after the war, reflecting on his time there. But in real life, O'Brien only has two sons. Referring to his book, O'Brien states, "Even though I knew it would be largely invented I wanted to make it feel true in the literal sense, real as if when we're reading a memoir, a work of nonfiction." When I teach the novel to my AP Literature classes, their frustration after learning this information shows O'Brien was successful. They, for the most part, want it to be true. They are frustrated to learn it's entirely fiction. Some can't get past it.

In teaching the novel, I often refer to big "T" Truth vs. little "t" truth. It's a way of explaining O'Brien's approach, and it's captured in the chapter "How to Tell a True War Story." Big "T" truths are more important than facts or details—they matter. Little "t" truths are facts and details that might be interesting to know or look up, but their accuracy doesn't make the story any

---

1. O'Brien, *The Things They Carried*, 83.

less important. This idea is captured when O'Brien outlines the trademarks of a "true war story." The one we spend the most time discussing is as follows: "You can tell a true war story by the questions you ask. Somebody tells a story, let's say, and afterwards you ask, 'Is it true?' and if the answer matters, you've got your answer." It's an initially confusing statement that becomes more and more clear as you apply it to the book.

And this is the line that jumped into my memory at church on Sunday. Our pastor was talking about the flood and was explaining a bit about exegesis and how there are different levels to understanding Hebrew texts. The first level, *pshat*, looks at plain meaning (or, as I would describe it: little "t" truth) and ties to the question "Did that happen?" The second level, *remez*, gets to symbolic meeting (or big "T" truth) and asks "Does that happen?" Again, it's initially a confusing concept, but it becomes more and more clear as you apply it.

Where did Noah get the materials to build a boat the length of a football field, and did any of it survive? Did the flood cover the whole earth or just the inhabited sections? How did Noah get two of every animal onto the boat—and what did they eat for forty days and forty nights? These are interesting questions—and they may spur research and discussion—but they aren't details that make or break my faith in God. They are *pshat*-level questions that don't get to the *remez* or big "T" truth.

On the other hand, does humanity continually fall short of what God calls us to do? Does God have the power to destroy his creation in a worldwide flood? And does our amazing God keep his covenant to never turn his back on us, no matter how often we disappoint him or break his commands? If those answers matter, you've got your answer.

> But when he, the Spirit of truth, comes, he will guide you into all the truth. He will not speak on his own; he will speak only what he hears, and he will tell you what is yet to come. (John 16:13, NIV)

You Shall Be Free Indeed

> Wanda turned to him. "Do you feel free? Do you know what free feels like?"
>
> How to explain his country to her, he wondered. How to explain that leaving its confines to sail upon the Sea of Japan—that was being free.
>
> "When you're in my country," he said, "everything makes simple, clear sense. It's the most straightforward place on earth."[1]
>
> —ADAM JOHNSON, *THE ORPHAN MASTER'S SON*

The main character in this novel, Jun Do, lives in North Korea. He has no freedom whatsoever. It is appalling to read this book and realize how the simplest "givens" in the Western world are not even within the realm of imagination for the citizens of North Korea. At the point in the story where this quote appears, Jun Do has been sent on a fake mission to Texas, of all places, to gather information for his country. It is a culture shock, to put it mildly. When the American journalist Wanda, in a private moment, asks him if he knows "what free feels like," he can only think of those moments where he has had a moment to himself, or where he crossed a boundary and realized he was no longer located on North Korean territory, as was the case now.

Interestingly, the Americans in Texas pronounce his name "John Doe." He doesn't understand why they think it's amusing until his host tells him that John Doe is "the name you give a missing person." Then the Texan corrects herself: "Actually, a John Doe is not a missing person. I think it's when you have the person, just not his

---

1. Johnson, *The Orphan Master's Son*, 154.

identity." And the journalist, Wanda, chimes in, "A John Doe has an exact identity. It's just yet to be discovered."[2]

Perhaps this is the author's way of telling us that this main character—this orphan, this nobody, this "unfree" young man—is "everyman," that is, he represents all of us. Like Jun Do, we are not free, not even those of us who live in a democracy. When people say, "It's a free country," they usually mean that we can do whatever we please, so don't get in our way. But of course, *that's* hardly true. When parents tell their children, "You can be anything you want to be when you grow up," that's not true either. We are confined by what we are good at, by the opportunities that come our way, and especially by the intellect and physique our genes have given us.

So ask yourself Wanda's question: "Do you know what free feels like?" Initially, we may think of exciting, escape-from-the-routine adventures as a worthy response. What is freedom? It's white water rafting, cliff diving, getting out of school for the summer, breaking away from authority in a small or large way. But of course, those are just temporary. One way or another, confinement is a part of our reality.

When some of the Jews asked Jesus about freedom, he responded, "If the Son sets you free, you will be free indeed." One of the most beautiful and perplexing paradoxes Christianity offers us is this: to be free, truly free, we must bind ourselves to Christ. Then it becomes clear to us that we are not in control, and this comes as a relief (another lovely paradox). Perhaps the best definition of real freedom is this: freedom is living in the space you were designed for. That space is the realm of God's love. As St. Augustine so eloquently said, "Thou hast made us for Thyself, O Lord, and our hearts are restless until they rest in Thee."[3] This is what it means to be both free and human. We all remain John Does in search of our identities until the Son sets us free.

> Jesus said, "If you hold to my teaching, you are really my disciples. Then you will know the truth, and the truth will set you free." (John 8:31–32, NIV)

2. Ibid., 140.

3. Augustine, *The Confessions*, ix.

The Truth About Gold

Nature's first green is gold,
Her hardest hue to hold.
Her early leaf's a flower;
But only so an hour.
So leaf subsides to leaf.
So Eden sank to grief,
So dawn goes down to day.
Nothing gold can stay.[1]

—ROBERT FROST, "NOTHING GOLD CAN STAY"

The first time I encountered this poem was in an American Literature class. The professor took our class for a stroll across the beautiful college campus. It was early spring, and he told us to look, really look around us as he recited this, one of his favorite poems, to us. Robert Frost's words rang with a truth that only the *experience* of witnessing "nature's first green" could offer.

Like my professor, I committed the poem to memory. And when I became a teacher, I included it on the syllabus of my Modern Poetry class. The students were required to take a certain number of "mini courses" like this one in order to graduate. Some who signed up were clearly poetry lovers. Others were putting in their time. One student in particular comes to mind. His name was Tom. He was the son of a dairy farmer, and he had no intention of going on to college as he loved the farm and wanted to get his high school diploma and join his father as soon as possible. When I introduced this course, he challenged me, a second-year teacher, by asking a semi-rude but sincere question: "What's the good of poetry, anyway?" I was taken aback but had the wherewithal to

1. Frost, *The Poetry of Robert Frost*, 222.

postpone an answer, saying I would think about that question seriously and give him my best answer the next day.

And I did think long and hard about it. The best answer I could come up with was this: "Sometimes we need poets to give us the words for the important things we cannot adequately express ourselves." I thought it was a pretty good comeback; Tom, however, shrugged, clearly unconvinced.

But six or seven years later, after I had left that school and moved to another city, I got a letter from Tom. He wrote that he was now running his dad's farm, that in fact, it was *his* farm now because his dad had dropped dead of a heart attack on the floor of the barn early one morning. And he ended the letter with these words, which are precious to me both as a human being and as a teacher: "And believe it or not, at his funeral all of a sudden I thought of a line from one of the poems you taught us—'nothing gold can stay.'"

Life offers us a lot of gold. There is the literal gold of a sunset, but there are also the golden moments of friendship, the first kiss, a newborn baby, a sweet victory against a rival team, and much more. But the sun sinks below the horizon, and friends wander away or are taken from us, and there is only one real *first* kiss; newborn babies grow up into rebellious adolescents, and the rival team wins the next time. This is the essence of the curse of Eden—that nothing beautiful lasts forever. It is the curse of loss, of separation. Nothing gold can stay.

With one exception: the love of God. And that glorious truth gives us a way to dry our tears, delight in the joys of life—however transient—and trust that the best is yet to come. The glorious gold of his love will never tarnish nor fade. This is God's promise to all those whose yearning hearts turn in his direction when the world lets us down. And we will not be disappointed.

> In this world you will have trouble. But take heart! I have overcome the world. (John 16:33, NIV)

Sin and Forgiveness

Who? Me?

> Miss Strangeworth moved slightly at the grocery counter to make room for Mrs. Harper.
>
> "Morning, Adela," Mrs. Harper said.
>
> And Miss Strangeworth said, "Good morning, Martha."
>
> "Ran out of sugar for my cake frosting," Mrs. Harper explained. Her hand shook slightly as she opened her pocketbook. Miss Strangeworth wondered, glancing at her quickly, if she had been taking proper care of herself.[1]
>
> —SHIRLEY JACKSON, "THE POSSIBILITY OF EVIL"

There are several characteristics of Shirley Jackson's short stories that make them appealing to the reader. The first is her ability to shock or surprise us by the end of a story, usually by her clever use of irony. The second is her insight into the darker side of human nature. And the third is her exaggerated plot, which I suspect she implements in order to, as Flannery O'Connor once wrote about her own short stories, "paint very large pictures"[2] so that people sit up and pay attention.

This story is particularly dark. One sees the main character, Miss Strangeworth, the town's dearest and oldest citizen, running errands in her beloved town and then returning home to fix herself lunch. She encounters several people along the way, making pleasant conversation with them. She takes note of the fact that her friend, Martha Harper is out of sorts. When she finally returns home she decides to write some of her "special" letters before rewarding herself with a delicious, carefully-prepared, light lunch. Most of her letters are written with a gold-frosted fountain

---

1. Jackson, "The Possibility of Evil," *American Gothic*, 80.
2. Edmundson, *A Political Companion to Flannery O'Connor*, 185.

pen, using perfect penmanship. But for her "special" letters, Miss Strangeworth uses a "dull stub of pencil" and writes them in a "childish block print." After going to the grocery store and seeing her friend Martha Harper, Miss Strangeworth prepares to send her second "special" letter to her friend. After careful consideration, she writes in a childish scrawl: "Have you found out yet what they were all laughing about after you left Thursday? Or is the wife really the last one to know?"

Miss Strangeworth does not sign this letter or any of the others like it that she sends regularly. These letters are sent to warn her friends and neighbors of the "possibility of evil" that is lurking in her beloved town. She doesn't really *know* if Martha's husband is unfaithful, but someone suggested it. She tells herself that "as long as evil existed unchecked in the world, it was her duty to keep her town alert to it. . . . There were so many wicked people in the world."[3]

The irony, of course, is that Miss Strangeworth is perhaps the most evil person in town, causing all kinds of anxiety and quarreling and fear by writing her letters. And the end of this shocking story reveals just how ugly the world can be.

If one is honest, it becomes evident that Shirley Jackson is not gently nudging us; she is actually twisting our arm to point out the darkness in each of us. Although most ordinary people do not go to the lengths Miss Strangeworth does to address the possibility of evil, all of us *do* judge others, often quickly and unfairly. We are so adept at spotting and pointing out the wrongs that we see around us and yet so generously forgiving of our own shortcomings—if we notice them at all. As C.S. Lewis once wrote to his brother, Warnie, "Aim at your neighbor's good in the same way as you aim at your own good. Now, you don't love yourself because of your own lovable qualities. . . . Even when you dislike yourself, you still wish for your own happiness. This is natural to one's own self—towards others it has to be worked on."[4]

---

3. Jackson, "The Possibility of Evil," *American Gothic*, 80.

4. Lewis, *Yours, Jack: Spiritual Direction from C.S. Lewis*, 77.

Be kind and compassionate to one another, forgiving each other, just as in Christ God forgave you. (Ephesians 4:32, NIV)

Selling One's Soul

"What proof have I that all you have been telling me is true?" said Tom.

"There's my signature," said the devil, pressing his finger on Tom's forehead.

So saying, the devil turned off among the thickets of the swamp, and seemed to go down, down, down, into the earth until nothing but his head and shoulders could be seen, and so on, until he totally disappeared.

When Tom reached home he found the black print of a finger, burned, as it were, into his forehead, which nothing could obliterate.[1]

—Washington Irving, "The Devil and Tom Walker"

In the story "The Devil and Tom Walker," Washington Irving creates a miserly, heartless character named Tom Walker who is willing to give his soul to the devil in order to become a rich man. As the deal is completed, Tom asks for some reassurance that he will really get what he has bargained for, and the devil "seals the deal," so to speak, by placing his finger upon his forehead. There he leaves his mark, which, interestingly, Tom can scrub to his heart's content but never erase.

For whatever reason, I always feel compelled to "flip over" this moment in the story with my students by presenting another "bargain" of sorts. This one takes place on Ash Wednesday, the beginning of Lent. At our church, we all go forward and receive from the pastor our ashes, which are lying in a small and unassuming wooden bowl. He puts two fingers into the soft substance and makes

1. Irving, "The Devil and Tom Walker," *The Legend of Sleepy Hollow and Other Stories, Or, The Sketchbook of Geoffrey Crayon, Gent*, 20.

the mark of a fat, clumsy cross on my forehead and says, "Repent, and believe in the gospel." And I feel a mixture of awe and laughter inside. I stand back in place and watch others go forward. A child in his mother's arms receives the mark, and so does his mother. As they depart, he holds her cheeks in his chubby hands and looks at her mark and smiles. A non-believer would find it silly, and it *does* look a bit silly—all these people consenting to this strange kind of makeup. "Fools," the unbeliever might utter, shaking his head. And he would be right. Beginning this journey with dirt on our foreheads, we revere a symbol of execution, admitting in a world that increasingly denies such things that we are just dust and ashes, that we desperately need forgiving. We are God's fools. And because we are his, we look at one another and smile.

Unlike Tom Walker, I *can* obliterate the mark on my forehead with a simple shower. But like him, I have made a contract—what Christians call a covenant—that is weighty beyond the telling. In whose hands will we trust the priceless care of our mortal souls?

> What good will it be for a man if he gains the whole world, yet forfeits his soul? (Matthew 16:26, NIV)

That "Dirty" Word

> After carefully placing two more blocks of peat on the fire,
> he stood for a long time watching the stretched canvas, but it
> seemed to billow naturally with the wind. At last he prayed,
> and got in under his blankets and closed his smoke-smarting
> eyes. On the inside of the bed, next to the wall, he could feel
> with his hand the comfortable piece of lead pipe.[1]

—WALTER VAN TILBURG CLARK, "THE PORTABLE PHONOGRAPH"

Back in the 1950s, people were conscious of the fact that the
world had very recently survived not one, but two world wars.
The damage done by each was inestimable, and the creation and
use of a nuclear bomb by the end of the second world war left everyone more than a little terrified at what we were capable of. In
the short story "The Portable Phonograph," written in the 1950s,
Walter Van Tilburg Clark paints a grey, dismal landscape. Clearly
a really terrible war has destroyed most of the homes and people
on the face of the earth, and those who survived have to find
some kind of shelter for themselves and whatever few possessions
and supplies they might still have.

One man, Dr. Jenkins, has apparently discovered a few other
survivors and has decided to practice hospitality in this unlikely
setting. He shares with them a reading from one of the books he
has managed to save—he only has four: Shakespeare, *Moby Dick*,
The Divine Comedy, and the Bible. The three guests are not given
names. You know two of them by their longings—one is dying
to write, and another, a musician, is dying to hear the strains of
music once again. The musician is the youngest guest present,
and he is clearly not well.

---

1. Clark, "The Portable Phonograph," 199.

On this night, the good doctor generously plays a record for them on his portable phonograph. Because a musician is present, the doctor allows him to make the choice. All of the men are transfixed by the hauntingly sad and elegant nocturne by Debussy, but the musician is almost agonized by its beauty. When the men depart to their own shelters, with many thanks, the good doctor is about to go to sleep, but first he carefully hides the phonograph. Then he lies down to try to sleep, holding a lead pipe in his hand.

Upon finishing the story, the reader will probably wonder about two things: why the story closes with a man sleeping with a lead pipe, and why the author uses the adjective "comfortable" to describe that pipe. Clearly, he is suggesting that the man feels he needs a weapon to guard his treasures. Perhaps the word "comfortable" is meant to imply that he cannot rest without feeling the reassuring weight of a weapon in his hand. Of course, this is a sad irony, since Dr. Jenkins is reminding us all that even after we see the devastation of what war has done, we are ready and willing to participate in another one, even on a small scale.

There is an unpopular word for the reason why this is so: *depravity*. It has been defined as what the Heidelberg Catechism calls "the evil that constantly clings to us"[2]—the consequence of the sin of Adam and Eve. We are unable to completely refrain from evil. The famous hymn "Come Thou Fount" says it well:

> *Prone to wander, Lord I feel it,*
> *Prone to leave the God I love . . .* [3]

It's not a popular belief. People want to believe that we can perfect our flaws and conquer the things that divide us. The word "sin" is used less and less to describe what goes wrong in the world today, but even the sophisticated *New York Times* columnist David Brooks writes in his book *The Road to Character*: "No matter how hard we try to replace sin with non-moral words, like 'mistake' or 'error' or 'weakness,' the most essential parts of life are matters of individual responsibility and moral choice. . . . The concept of sin

2. Bierma, *The Theology of the Heidelberg Catechism*, 198.
3. Robinson, "Come Thou Fount of Every Blessing," 521.

is necessary because it is radically true. To say you are a sinner is to say that, like the rest of us, you have some perversity in your nature. We want to do one thing, but we end up doing another. We want what we should not want."[4]

If we are willing to admit to our fallen state, we can understand two important things. First, we will recognize that struggling against sin means recognizing that every day we have to work at choosing good over evil, even in something as tiny as finding a waste receptacle for trash instead of tossing it to the ground for someone else to deal with. Second, we will see our need for a sinless savior, someone who can deliver us from ourselves.

> For what I do is not the good I want to do; no, the evil I do
> not want to do—this I keep on doing. (Romans 7:19, NIV)

4. Brooks, *The Road to Character*, 54.

Less Is More

Ransom turned to the tree.... Each of the bright spheres
[hanging from it]... were not fruit at all but bubbles....
And looking round he perceived innumerable shimmer-
ing globes of the same kind in every direction. He began
to examine the nearest one attentively.... Moved by a natural impulse he put out his hand to touch it. Immediately
his head, face, and shoulders were drenched with what
seemed (in this warm world) an ice-cold shower bath,
and his nostrils filled with a sharp, shrill, exquisite scent.
... Such was the refreshment that he seemed to himself
to have been, till now, half awake.... All the colors about
him seemed richer and the dimness of that world seemed
clarified.... Looking at a fine cluster of the bubbles which
hung above his head he thought how easy it would be to
plunge oneself through the whole lot of them and to feel
at once that magical refreshment multiplied ten-fold. But
he restrained himself.[1]

—C.S. LEWIS, PERELANDRA

Perelandra is the planet Venus in C.S. Lewis' second book of his
science fiction trilogy. Ransom has come here for a purpose only
God knows, and as he searches for answers, Ransom discovers that
Perelandra is a paradise, a perfect place, similar to the Garden of
Eden before the fall. The bubble trees are just one sampling of how
incredibly lush and inviting this planet is. Touch one gently and
you are given a cold shower that makes you feel years younger,
invigorated beyond anything you have ever known, and more at-
tuned to color and smell than you ever dreamed possible.

1. Lewis, *Perelandra*, 43.

But Lewis makes a point of saying that Ransom, even though he would love to multiply the pleasure of this bubble shower many times over, *restrains* himself from doing so. Why? It is such a positive experience—why not repeat it? The answer to that question lies in a word that needs some polishing off in our vocabulary since it is no longer used or even acknowledged very often. The word is *temperance*.

What is temperance? Well, it is one of the cardinal virtues according to the Catholic church. It means exercising self-restraint, especially in regard to the gratification of our appetites or passions. The seven cardinal virtues were often paired with a deadly sin, and the deadly sin that is paired with temperance is *gluttony*. We often associate gluttony, rightly, with food, but we lack moderation in many areas of life. The point is, people tend to take in more than they need. Ransom thinks to himself, "This itch to have things over again, as if life were a film that could be unrolled twice or even made to work backwards—was it possibly the root of all evil? No, the love of money was called that. But money itself—perhaps one valued it chiefly as a defense against chance, a security for being able to have things over again, a means of arresting the unrolling of the film."

Perhaps the ability to resist grasping for more is a way of enjoying more completely what we have been given. Perhaps the fact that we strive to increase the number of our pleasures hinders the pleasure at hand. We live in a world whose litany is "I want, I want, I want. . . ." Like Ransom, we need to allow ourselves the delight of the gift without looking for another.

> If you find honey, eat just enough—too much of it and you will vomit. (Proverbs 25:16, NIV)

Gracefully and Far and Deep

> He felt lighter inside, nothing left to hide. Thuan Yen was still there, of course, and always would be, but the horror was now outside him. Ugly and pitiful and public. No less evil, he thought, but at least the demands of secrecy were gone. Which was another of nature's sly tricks. Once you're found out, you don't tremble at being found out. The trapdoor drops open. All you can do is fall gracefully and far and deep.[1]
>
> —Tim O'Brien, *In the Lake of the Woods*

Tim O'Brien writes about war. The Vietnam War. And the stories aren't always pleasant reading. They are brutal and painful and provocative. And honest. O'Brien served in Vietnam. He knows what he's writing about. The stories aren't always true, but they are truthful.

Part of that truthfulness—the feeling of shame and guilt that might come with warfare—is explored in his novel *In the Lake of the Woods*. In it, the main character John Wade spends much of his life burying the truths of what he was involved with during Vietnam. The things he experienced, and the things O'Brien describes with painful verisimilitude, weren't easy to discuss; there would be consequences for sharing those experiences. So he hid them from everyone.

But often, there are consequences for not sharing experiences as well. Guilt and self-judgment weigh heavy on a sinner's heart. It's not easy to move beyond a bad choice, a poor decision, or a sinful act. Often, hiding an indiscretion causes more problems than letting it be known. Life becomes more difficult when carrying the weight of guilt. This is the case in John Wade's story. And it's a reality for many others as well.

1. O'Brien, *In the Lake of the Woods*, 247.

Thankfully, as Christians, we know we always have a listening, non-judgmental, and forgiving ear. God is always a prayer away from easing some of this weight and allowing us to begin healing. Pope Francis's Twitter account reminds us that "in Confession we encounter the merciful embrace of the Father. His love always forgives."[2] For those carrying the weight of guilt, a "merciful embrace" is a welcome image. And in *Wishful Thinking*, Frederick Buechner explains, "To confess your sins to God is not to tell God anything God doesn't already know. Until you confess them, however, they are the abyss between you. When you confess them, they become the Golden Gate Bridge."[3]

And that bridge begins restoration. It restores the relationship the sinner has with God. Suddenly, the weight of sin feels lighter. It isn't always the final solution; however, it is the first and most important step and always ends in forgiveness. After this initial confession, there might be people on earth who also deserve open and honest conversations and confessions for healing to become fully complete. And those conversations might not always be as grace-filled and forgiving, but they are also important. And when those conversations finally happen, they may allow, as O'Brien describes it, a trapdoor to drop open, the weight of sin to be fully lifted, and the sinner to fall, *gracefully* and far and deep.

> Therefore confess your sins to each other and pray for each other so that you may be healed. (James 5:16, NIV)

2. Francis, "Twitter / @Pontifex."
3. Buechner, *Wishful Thinking*, 18.

Rotting Bones

> I was not of the same quality as he. I couldn't stand this.
> . . . Holding firmly to the trunk, I took a step toward him,
> and then my knees bent and I jounced the limb. . . . Finny
> tumbled sideways, broke through the little branches below
> and hit the river bank with a sickening, unnatural thud.[1]
>
> —JOHN KNOWLES, *A SEPARATE PEACE*

Have you ever wished for someone else's life? Perhaps you came to high school with some high expectations regarding how you would fare in the social or academic or fine arts or sports arena and soon realized that although you may have been fairly successful in middle school, the "playing field" got a lot more competitive in high school. You watched the seeming ease with which so many others enter into things, and you got discouraged. In fact, if you are at all ambitious—let's face it—you felt downright envious.

Such is the case for Gene Forrester in *A Separate Peace.* His roommate at a boys' prep school during WWII is a young man named Phineas (Finny). Phineas possesses what might be called glamorous powers; his ability to shine in any sport and his natural charisma in any social situation make him an unchallenged, popular leader. And although Gene considers himself Phineas' friend—in fact, his best friend—he is privately consumed by envy and resentment. It finally results in Gene purposely jouncing the tree limb Phineas is perched upon during a jumping contest Phineas has dreamed up for the boys' free time. The result is disastrous—for Phineas and Gene.

Long ago the writer Victor Hugo wrote a poem personifying Envy. One of the gods offers Envy anything she wants with the provision that her sister, Avarice, gets a double portion of her wish.

---

1. Knowles, *A Separate Peace*, 60.

Envy really struggles with this prospect, obviously—what good is getting your heart's desire if another not only receives it but receives twice as much of it? Finally, though, she makes a decision, and with a "malignant sneer," she proclaims, "I want to be blind in one eye."[2]

Envy is one of the seven deadly sins. What makes it so deadly is that at the root of envy is a lack of gratitude. Instead of rejoicing in the gifts we *do* possess, we resent those who have the ones we don't. If we live without gratitude we are spitting in the face of the giver of all good gifts, and it eats away at our ability to find pleasure in the potential good that lies before and within us.

Such thinking is incredibly narcissistic. The world does not revolve around us, despite all the media messages we hear to the contrary. In freely and generously celebrating the gifts and accomplishments of others, we demonstrate humility and grace, and in the process, we not only build community but more importantly become more Christ-like. This requires a cultivated mindset, since it is natural to desire praise and recognition; the hard work of building shalom and being grateful to the Creator is our highest calling. In his famous *Screwtape Letters,* C.S. Lewis puts it plainly: "[God] wants each man, in the long run, to be able to recognize all creatures (even himself) as glorious and excellent things. . . . His whole effort, therefore, will be to get the man's mind off the subject of his own value altogether."[3]

> A heart at peace gives life to the body, but envy rots the bones. (Proverbs 14:30, NIV)

2. Hugo, *The Complete Poems of Victor Hugo*, 5.
3. Lewis, *The Screwtape Letters*, 64-65.

Remember

I sat against one of the house's clay walls. The kinship I
felt suddenly for the old land. . . it surprised me. I'd been
gone long enough to forget and be forgotten. I had a home
in a land that might as well be in another galaxy to the
people sleeping on the other side of the wall I leaned
against. I thought I had forgotten about this land. But I
hadn't. And under the bony glow of a half-moon, I sensed
Afghanistan humming under my feet. Maybe Afghanistan
hadn't forgotten me either.[1]

—KHALED HOSSEINI, *THE KITE RUNNER*

The Kite Runner is an intense, intriguing story about a young boy
named Amir who grows up in Afghanistan in a privileged family. His best friend is a young houseboy named Hassan. Despite
the incredibly close bond between them, Amir eventually tries to
forget Hassan because Amir cruelly betrays his loyal, brave friend.
Amir and his father flee to America, but he only *thinks* he has put
his past behind him; when he returns to Afghanistan as an adult,
he allows his memories of Hassan to return to him. And so, unconsciously, he begins his journey toward forgiving himself.

Perhaps you have had the experience of something you
thought you had forgotten finding its way back into your memory.
A song, perhaps. Have you ever heard a song on the radio that
immediately returns you to an event that happened a long time
ago? Isn't it strange how you slip back to your memories of that
event—and its emotions—as you listen? Or maybe you come upon
an old letter that someone wrote you back in middle school or a
picture you drew in elementary school, and for just a moment you
breathe in that time frame once again. Perhaps, like Amir, you have

---

1. Hosseini, *The Kite Runner*, 240.

some things you would rather forget. Old failures. Mistakes. Injustices. A death. And yet they come back to us. I remember after our son died of cancer, I came upon the red baseball cap that he wore almost every day on his bald little head. It fell off a high shelf in the closet and landed at my feet, and I was surprised at how quickly I was brought back into the land of grief.

When I used to teach eighth grade Bible, I asked my students to draw what the writer Frederick Buechner calls "a Room called Remember."[2] The idea behind the assignment was to construct a room that holds all those things or people or even just words that were somehow formative. The finished products amazed me. One girl drew a variety of people wandering about in her room, and then in one closet she drew a picture of a very old lady she had only met (significantly) once. Another student painted the word SHAME all over one wall in red. Other students' rooms included things like trophies, a worn baby blanket, a hockey stick, a viola, books, an easel. Some of them had tombstones, and one that I recall had dark little clouds over everything he drew because he had suffered from depression for a long time before it was diagnosed. Located somewhere important in the character Amir's "room called Remember" there would surely be a kite.

Remembering is especially important in the life of a Christian. It gives us insight not only into where we have been, but also into where we may be heading. When Jesus met with his disciples near the end of his life, he asked them to remember him every time they broke the bread and drank the wine of Passover. When he broke the bread that night, he asked his disciples to let it forever after remind them of the time when his body was broken. And as he raised the cup of wine, he asked them forever after to let it remind them of the time when his blood was shed. So in our churches today, the sacrament of communion is a deliberate act of remembering.

Remembering is a great gift, however painful at times. It is my hope and prayer for all of us that in the center of our individual "rooms called Remember" we will deliberately place a cup,

2. Buechner, *A Room Called Remember*, 3.

a loaf of bread, and a cross—all symbols of death, which Christ has conquered. All symbols of life, which he offers in abundance. *Remember* and believe—it is the only way we can find forgiveness and healing.

> The Lord Jesus, on the night he was betrayed, took bread, and when he had given thanks, he broke it and said, "This is my body, which is for you; do this in remembrance of me." In the same way, after supper he took the cup, saying, "This cup is the new covenant in my blood; do this, whenever you drink it, in remembrance of me." (1 Corinthians 11:24–25, NIV)

Restraint

> There is nothing that keeps wicked men at any one mo-
> ment out of hell, but the mere pleasure of God.[1]
>
> —Jonathan Edwards, "Sinners in the Hands of
> an Angry God"

In almost any American literature anthology, you will be likely to
find that the Puritan era is represented by an excerpt of this sermon
by Jonathan Edwards. I think that there are two reasons for this.
First, the figures of speech implemented by Edwards are vivid and
disturbing. And second, the sermon seems to affirm all the negative
modern-day interpretations of Puritan belief.

Probably the three strongest figures of speech in this sermon
are a bow and arrow, a great dam of floodwaters, and a spider
hanging from a thread:

> "The bow of God's wrath is bent and the arrow made
> ready on the string, and justice bends the arrow at your
> heart and strains the bow."
>
> "The wrath of God is like great waters that are
> dammed. . . . If God should only withdraw His hand
> from the floodgate, it would immediately fly open."
>
> "God holds you over the pit of hell, much as one
> holds a spider. . . . You hang by a slender thread."

All of these conjure up frightening images for us, probably especially for modern-day readers who have rarely (if ever) heard a sermon
on hell. Why is that? My students say that the reason is we have
become enlightened and recognize now that God is a God of love,
not judgment. Who wants a God like the one Edwards presents?
And I think they are probably correct in that assessment, although
I firmly believe that we have lost something of great significance

1. Edwards, "Sinners in the Hands of an Angry God," 321.

by emphasizing only the other end of the spectrum. God is both a God of love and a God of judgment. This combination may not be the God we want, but it is the God we get. And we should be glad of this. How can we fully know or appreciate his grace and love if we do not see how badly we need it? We cheapen grace, and especially its price tag, if we do not see, as the Heidelberg Catechism suggests, the weight of "our sins and miseries."[2]

But here is my second point. The sermon *seems* to affirm a negative view of God. But really, it does not. Think about it. The bow is bent, and the arrow is pointed at your heart—but has the arrow been released? The waters are dammed by God's mighty hand, and he has not released the floodgates. The spider dangles over the fires of hell, and God is the one holding onto the other end of the thread. God's restraint comes from his great mercy and love for us.

C.S. Lewis once said that one of the great successes of the devil was convincing people like you and me that Puritan is a dirty word. We have twisted it to suggest that the idea of being temperate (restrained) is the same as being legalistic, being chaste (pure) is prudish, being sober (serious) is depressing, and feeling guilty (repentant) indicates uptightness. But the complete, hard, and beautiful truth is this: "Amazing grace, how sweet the sound / that saved a *wretch* like me."[3]

> So I find this law at work: When I want to do good, evil is right there with me. . . . What a wretch I am! Who will rescue me from this body of death? Thanks be to God—through Jesus Christ our Lord!" (Romans 7:21, 23–24, NIV)

2. Bierma, *The Theology of the Heidelberg Catechism*, 13.

3. Wesley, "Amazing Grace," 691.

Discernment

Taking Note

so much depends
upon

a red wheel
barrow

glazed with rain
water

beside the white
chickens[1]

—WILLIAM CARLOS WILLIAMS, "THE RED WHEELBARROW"

When I introduce imagism to my American Literature students, they have much the same reaction one sees in a museum of art where the average person viewing a Rothko painting of four shades of red exclaims: "Really? *I* could do that!"

But the imagist has a very important but simple task—to point at something specific and put a frame around it. He need not comment much—simply setting it off from the rest of the ordinary world for the moment is what matters. The "so much depends" is a drum roll of sorts, albeit a quiet one. Take a moment to really *look at* these three unremarkable things because for *someone* they matter a great deal.

When my students actually have to attempt their own imagistic poems, they see how difficult it can actually be. One year,

1. Williams, "The Red Wheelbarrow," *Poetry for Young People*, 27.

shortly after a student in our class had died, one of my students wrote this poem:

> A chair does not
> speak
> smile
> cry
> will never laugh.
> That is why
> tears
>
> fall.

I *saw*, from his spare words, the empty chair that haunted me for the remainder of the semester. One of the most important things we are called to do with the lives we are given is to take note of the significance of things, to be open to what beauty or sorrow or small goodness they have to offer.

> See how the lilies of the field grow. They do not labor or spin. Yet I tell you that not even Solomon in all his splendor was dressed like one of these. (Matthew 6:28–29, NIV)

Brain and Heart Hacking

> My father said, "Truth is a hard deer to hunt. If you eat
> too much truth at once, you may die of the truth." He was
> right—it is better the truth should come little by little. . . .
> Perhaps in the old days, they ate knowledge too fast."[1]
>
> —Stephen Vincent Benet, "By the Waters of Babylon"

Recently on CBS's *60 Minutes*, Anderson Cooper interviewed a former Google product manager named Tristan Harris. Harris, con-
cerned for the future of young people particularly, had the courage
to speak out on some of his concerns regarding the long-term consequences of phone technology. Harris says, "Every time I check my
phone, I'm playing the slot machine to see 'What did I get?' This is
one way to hijack people's minds and create an addictive habit." The
result, he claims, is increased anxiety, loss of focus on the matter at
hand, and an addictive, dependent lifestyle. He calls this technique
on the part of creators of technology "brain hacking."[2]

In the short story "By the Waters of Babylon," written way
back in the 1930s, Stephen Vincent Benet warns us of basically
the same thing. We are introduced in the story to a primitive society; the reader is surprised to learn that this is actually a *modern,
post-apocalyptic* world which is struggling to survive after what the
priest calls "The Great Burning" took place many years before. The
priest's son goes off on a quest to discover what this world was like
and is given a vision of great highways, tall buildings, modern conveniences, and one solitary figure gazing out from the window of
his office with a look of great sadness on his face. The boy does not
understand. He returns to his father and asks, "What happened?"

---

1. Benet, "By the Waters of Babylon," 68.
2. "Brain Hacking."

And his father's reply has a prophetic significance for today's reader. He says, "They ate knowledge too fast."

I am amazed at how often people hearing about difficult situations occurring in the world today respond by saying something along the lines of, "Well, we have to find the technology which will help us resolve these issues." Our new slogan seems to be "in technology we trust"—a grave error. One of the most ironic times I heard this confident faith in technology expressed was shortly after the global hacking which basically shut down computers over most of the world, causing hospitals to go into crisis and the loss of valuable information in major companies. I would be one of the first to celebrate some of the wonderful gifts technology has given us, but in the same breath I can mourn the things which technology has taken from us.

Our responsibility as Christians in this world is to discern the pace and value of the knowledge we pursue and digest. Are there roads we should not go down? Can we ever use the word "enough" in regard to not only our improved products but also our devotion to them? It takes courage and wisdom to evaluate our dependence on the multitude of gadgets and sophisticated technological advances that are constantly being dangled before us. But this is what it means to be responsible caretakers of the world God has given us.

> It is not good to have zeal without knowledge, nor to be hasty and miss the way. (Proverbs 19:2, NIV)

Definitely Not Safe

> "I was just thinking: what if we could hold up things that were bright red, or bright yellow, and he could *choose?* Instead of the sameness."
>
> "He might make wrong choices."
>
> "Oh." Jonas was silent for a minute. "Oh, I see what you mean. It wouldn't matter for a newchild's toy. But later it *does* matter, doesn't it? We don't dare to let people make choices of their own."
>
> "Not safe?" The Giver suggested.
>
> "Definitely not safe," Jonas said with certainty.[1]
>
> —Lois Lowry, *The Giver*

Imagine a world without choice: jobs awarded with mandatory training beginning at age twelve, marriages decided by a Committee of Elders, and children dispersed to couples at an appropriate time in their relationship. This is exactly the scenario Lois Lowry's *The Giver* depicts.

And in some ways, it's not all bad. Things seem to work well for the residents in her fictional world. Jobs are carefully chosen for each individual based on their abilities and what's necessary for their economy. For children who show empathy toward the elderly, there's a career as "Caretaker of the Old." For children who seem astute at mathematics and science, a job in engineering. And for the youngster that can't stay serious and focused? The Director of Recreation has a position waiting. Marriages are also predetermined, and when a married couple feels ready for parenting,

---

1. Lowry, *The Giver*, 98.

children are placed in homes deemed appropriate for child, parent, and the overall population.

Yet, as is typical in science fiction, things aren't exactly ideal either. In order to maintain stability in society, even the smallest of choices are completely removed. One consequence of abolishing options is that feelings are streamlined so no one experiences extremes in either direction. There is no fear of failure or defeat in finding or working at an occupation, but there is also no exuberance at having succeeded or having been given a promotion for a job well done. The negative feelings of heartbreak and jealousy in relationships are gone, but so are passion and love. Lowry's book shows us that although poor choices may, at times, result in pain and difficulty, great choices bring even more joy as a result. The absence of choice is safer but also less satisfying.

This is not a consequence our all-knowing God wants us to face. The first book of the Bible explains how mankind was given choice. God could have created us as unthinking and programmed followers, but he left us with a choice—and we get to choose to follow him or deny him. Genesis explains how we chose incorrectly. And we continue to choose incorrectly, and the heartbreak, failure, jealousy, and defeat that comes with those incorrect choices hurts us. God's decision to give us choice was definitely "not safe."

But it also gives us the opportunity to truly appreciate (to borrow the phrasing from Philip Yancey) what's so amazing about grace. Our poor choices make God's gift to us even more fulfilling. Yancey explains how "grace means there is nothing I can do to make God love me more, and nothing I can do to make God love me less. It means that I, even I who deserve the opposite, am invited to take my place at the table in God's family."[2] No matter how often we make incorrect choices, we are always granted the opportunity to make another choice—the choice to accept the amazing gift of grace. And when followers make that choice, there is a resulting joy that couldn't be achieved by keeping things safe.

2. Yancey, *What's So Amazing About Grace?*, 71.

But if serving the Lord seems undesirable to you, then choose for yourselves this day whom you will serve, whether the gods your ancestors served beyond the Euphrates, or the gods of the Amorites, in whose land you are living. But as for me and my household, we will serve the Lord. (Joshua 24:15, NIV)

The Eye That Blinks

What does it mean to have to suffer so much if our lives
are nothing more than the blink of an eye? I learned a
long time ago that a blink of an eye in itself is nothing.
But the eye that blinks, *that* is something. A span of life is
nothing. But the man who lives that span, *he* is something.
He can fill that tiny span with meaning, so its quality is
immeasurable though its quantity may be insignificant.
Do you understand what I am saying? A man must fill his
life with meaning.[1]

—CHAIM POTOK, *THE CHOSEN*

In Chaim Potok's novel *The Chosen*, a teenage boy named Reuven
Malter fears for his father's life after he suffers a heart attack. He
knows that the reason for his father's poor health is primarily due
to the fact that he works too hard for the cause of Zionism—a cause
that has become his passion ever since he learned of the number
of Jewish people killed in the Holocaust in Europe. In response to
his son's concern, Mr. Malter offers him the wise words above. Put
simply, he wants his son to know that no matter how long (or short)
a person's life is, it must have meaning. Having heard Potok speak in
person a number of years ago, I believe that these words reflect his
own philosophy of life. In particular, I remember his emphasis on
the fact that life has meaning if a person has the courage to recognize suffering and then *do something* about it.

Let me switch gears slightly and talk about fame. Fame is
not what Mr. Malter is talking about when he says, "The eye that
blinks, that is something. . . . the man who lives that span, he is
something." But our world has increasingly come to the conclusion that fame *is* what makes us something, what gives our lives

1. Potok, *The Chosen*, 204.

significance. Supposedly the artist Andy Warhol once claimed that someday everyone would be famous for fifteen minutes. (Years later, David Bowie, in one of his songs, asked Warhol when Bowie would get his fifteen minutes.)

I suppose to some extent everyone wants that fifteen minutes as long as the fame makes us look good in some way. There are even some who will settle for fifteen minutes of infamy. Something in the human heart longs for recognition. You become a teacher, or a scientist or maybe an architect or soldier or politician. Regardless of your career choice, there is a part of you that hopes to "make a name for yourself"—to be that teacher who some famous actor thanks publicly on a talk show, or to be the scientist who discovers the cure for cancer, the architect who gets compared to Frank Lloyd Wright, the heavily-decorated soldier, the politician who made it all the way to Washington.

But that's not the point of Mr. Malter's words to his son. Each and every person's life has significance if what gets him or her up in the morning is the desire to make the world a better place. One of my son's favorite high school teachers used to say at the end of his first hour class every single day, "The whole day is ahead of you. You get to choose whether you're going to be a blessing or a curse today. I hope you choose the first one."

As a Christian, I will take this message a step further. Each and every person's life has significance simply because we were created in the image of God. When we die, we will eventually be forgotten—some sooner, some later. It doesn't really matter. What ultimately matters is two things: 1) what choices we made while we were here, large and small, and 2) the God of the universe knows us by name.

> Before I formed you in the womb, I knew you. (Jeremiah 1:5, NIV)

Mortal Stakes

My object in living is to unite
My avocation and my vocation
As my two eyes make one in sight.
Only where love and need are one,
And work is play for mortal stakes,
Is the deed ever really done
For heaven and the future's sakes.[1]

—ROBERT FROST, "TWO TRAMPS IN MUD TIME"

In the poem "Two Tramps in Mud Time," Robert Frost describes himself as a person who loves to chop wood as an "escape" from his usual work. Wielding his axe is a satisfying release of energy and emotion; he loses himself in the single-mindedness of a chore that feels more like play than work. But one day two tramps come wandering into his yard and ask him if *they* can chop his wood for him. And he resents it. They want to take away his play, call it work, and get paid for it.

This makes the poet ponder the difference between *avocation* and *vocation*. Avocation for Frost is spending time outside with his axe and a pile of wood. For you it might be taking a run or doing a puzzle. Avocation is *play*. Vocation, by contrast, is the work you *must* do to "make a living." Vocation is a career. The poet's struggle with these two tramps highlights the difference between these two words. Avocation is what we *love* to do. Vocation is what we *need* to do. And clearly "theirs [the tramps'] was the better right," Frost writes, because they have to survive, after all.

And that realization brings Frost a bit further to a lovely insight. In the best of all worlds, there is no distinction between

1. Frost, *The Poetry of Robert Frost*, 277.

avocation and vocation, love and need. We do the work that must be done a) because we are good at it, b) because it supplies our basic needs, and best of all c) *because we love doing it.*

How many jobs are like that? In your own consideration of a career, what are your biggest priorities? For many, sadly, the items at the top of the list are often two things: money and prestige. We want a vocation that makes our avocations boundlessly possible. We want a vocation that makes the rest of the world respect and notice us. But quite possibly, if those two considerations are at the top of the list, we might be miserable as we head off to work each day, counting the days until vacation. Frost is suggesting that if we choose work that we love and take delight in, we have made avocation a natural ingredient of vocation.

Frederick Buechner writes eloquently about this in his book *Wishful Thinking*: "Vocation is the place where our deep gladness meets the world's deep need."[2] And this is the call of God himself into our lives. The word *vocation*, after all, comes from the Latin *vocare*—literally, *to call.* If you are trying to figure out where you go from here—what path to pursue in your vocation—try considering the fact that God may be calling you to something that would not only make work "feel like play" but that could be work done for "mortal stakes." How do you discern this? Pay attention to the things that delight you. Listen to what people say you are good at—especially if you hear it more than once. They may be the messengers for God's call to you. And finally, pray for discernment. God will surely find a way to answer such prayers, for they are prayers that ask for the chance to be instrumental in the building of his kingdom.

> Whatever you do, work at it with all your heart, as work-
> ing for the Lord, not for men. (Colossians 3:23, NIV)

---

2. Buechner, *Wishful Thinking*, 95.

Lines and Circles

Esperanza.

The old woman with marble hands called me aside. She held my face with her blue-veined hands and looked and looked at me. A long silence.

When you leave you must remember always to come back, she said.

What?

When you leave you must remember to come back for the others. A circle, understand? You will always be Esperanza. You will always be Mango Street. You can't erase what you know. You can't forget who you are.[1]

—SANDRA CISNEROS, *THE HOUSE ON MANGO STREET*

Life can be lived in one of two ways, I suspect. The first way to live one's life is to live it like a timeline. You've probably seen plenty of timelines in history books. If you drew a timeline on the wall, you could put little markers on it to note certain key events. No doubt you could come up with some for your own life: your first steps, beginning school, moving to a new place, and the death or loss of someone you loved.

Esperanza is told by one of three strange, almost witch-like women that an important event is coming in her life. It is something she has longed for ever since she can remember: she will get to leave Mango Street. Mango Street, a street of poverty, of lost dreams and strange, often hopeless people. Mango Street, a place where the few who still dared to hope, mainly hoped to escape. She

---

1. Cisneros, *The House on Mango Street*, 105.

can hardly believe her ears—is it possible that she can finally put this depressing chapter in her life behind her?

Yes. But the old woman hasn't finished yet. She will leave, but she has to come back.

Which brings us to the second way to live one's life. Instead of a line—a circle. The thing about a line is that it keeps going. The thing about a circle is that it keeps returning. Living life as a circle is a wiser and harder choice. It demands that you *remember.* The old woman wasn't telling Esperanza she literally had to come back and live on Mango Street. She was telling her that Mango Street had shaped and taught her, and that returning to it—if only in her mind, if only in a book about that place—will not only give her the ability to make sense of it, but it could also help someone *else* to make sense of it.

You lose your best friend in a terrible accident. You try your hardest to get past it and get on with your life. When others bring it up, or when you see a movie that reminds you of it, you retreat as quickly as possible to spare yourself the pain.

That is living life as a line.

You lose your best friend in a terrible accident. You work through your grief. You meet others who have lost someone they love, and you willingly return to your pain in order to help them with theirs. That is living life as a circle.

The first is about self-preservation. The second is about empathy. As Christians, we are called to the latter. If you have any doubt about that, think about the ultimate example of empathy, Christ himself, who became one of us so that we can be reconciled to God.

> Each of you should look, not only to your own interests, but also to the interests of others. Your attitude should be the same as that of Christ Jesus. (Philippians 2:4–5a, NIV)

Yearning

Holy

> "Come on," the big man said, "let's have a look at his tattoo," and while Parker squirmed in their hands, they pulled up his shirt. Parker felt all the hands drop away instantly and his shirt fell again like a veil over the face. There was a silence in the room which seemed to Parker to grow from the circle around him until it extended to the foundations under the building and upward through the beams in the roof.[1]

—FLANNERY O'CONNOR, "PARKER'S BACK"

I love this story. I love the flawed, comical, desperate character of Parker and his quest for meaning and holiness in his disheveled life. Like the biblical Jonah, he runs from God, and like the reluctant prophet, he is found and forever changed.

Parker covers his body with tattoos, but they lack the pattern and symmetry of the man he saw in a fair as a youth. Parker's tattoos are random and impulsively chosen—an eagle, his mother's name on a heart (because it was the only way she would pay for it), an anchor, a tiger, a rifle. . .whatever struck his fancy. Soon, every part of his body is covered. Except his back.

For me, reading this story, the familiar phrase "I've got your back" oddly comes to mind. Parker does not put a tattoo on his back because, quite frankly, he can't ever see and appreciate it. But when circumstances bring him to the moment when he decides to put one there anyway, it is the face of Christ that he chooses as his tattoo, and reading the story you get the feeling that he has been claimed by something—no, someone—much bigger than him.

The above quote is the moment when Parker's newly-covered back gets exposed for the first time. He is in a bar, and when someone slaps him on the back and he winces in pain, they know

---

1. O'Connor, *The Complete Stories*, 526.

he has a new tattoo. Despite his protests, they pull off his shirt. And that is the most beautiful moment in the story. Because the whole room becomes silent. They are in the presence of holiness, and they are silent.

Frederick Buechner tells the story of seeing a small news clip in a movie theatre where the huge statue of Christ is placed on Corcovado Mountain in Rio de Janeiro. A helicopter is used to fly it in. Buechner says that from a distance, no one could make it out at first, but then gradually the crowd realizes what it is. "Hey look!" someone calls out. "It's a flying Jesus!" Everyone laughs, and more jokes are tossed out. But then the statue comes closer and closer, and the camera zooms in on the face. And the entire theatre is transformed into an eerie, respectful silence. The laughter and whistling die instantly. They are in the presence of holiness, and they are silent.[2]

Perhaps you have known such a time. Someone speaks from the heart in chapel or in the classroom, or simply over a cup of coffee, and the words are so honest and full of truth that those listening look down in silence. A sunset on the edge of the water, whose rays seem to dissipate into the water itself, and those watching have stopped chattering to let it somehow dissipate into them. A strain of music. . . an image on the television screen of a child caught in the hell of war. . . a compelling painting in a museum. . . a story that makes your heart beat faster or tears roll down your cheeks. . . . You find yourself without words because you are in the presence of holiness—God is choosing to contact you through all the noise and trivialities of your day, and he hopes you will pause and take it in. If you do, take note. Take note of your tears, of your quickly beating heart, and especially of the silence. For you are standing on holy ground.

> For God who said, "Let the light shine out of darkness,"
> made his light shine in our hearts to give us the light of
> the knowledge of the glory of God in the face of Christ.
> (2 Corinthians 4:6, NIV)

2. Buechner, *The Hungering Dark*, 11.

Practicing Resurrection

> She was dead. I understood that. After all, I'd seen her body, and yet even as a nine-year-old I had begun to practice the magic of stories. . . . And at nighttime I'd slide into sleep knowing that Linda would be there waiting for me.[1]
>
> —TIM O'BRIEN, *THE THINGS THEY CARRIED*

There are a rare few books in this world which have the power to transfix us—to make us sit and hold the book itself as we are reading it, pausing to let something really rich sink into us, making us grateful for its ability to reach deep into an unnamed place within us. *The Things They Carried* is such a book for me. It is the story of the Vietnam War. . . but really it is a story about death and life and trying to come to terms with both.

The quote above comes near the very end of the book. After all his stories about the men he fought with during the war, O'Brien seems to need to remind us that, as one of his friends says after spending all day loading up dead bodies in various stages of destruction and decomposition into a truck: "Death sucks." Indeed. Yet the death he describes here was not the death of a fellow soldier or an enemy, but his first, real, up close and personal encounter with death. Linda, his best friend from childhood, died of a brain tumor in the fourth grade. O'Brien writes that despite their youth and innocence, ". . . I know for a fact that what we felt for each other was as deep and rich as love can ever get."

I put down the book at this point before reading the final few pages and took a deep breath as I remembered something important from my own life. Two years after our seven-year-old son Adam died from cancer, his younger brother, Luke, age seven at the time, was looking for something to do one lazy summer afternoon. Luke told

---

1. O'Brien, *The Things They Carried*, 244.

me that he was working on a "big project," and I couldn't see it until it was finished. He occasionally raced into the house to get some item of clothing or some old rags, and I could hear the slight "bang" of the tool shed door from time to time. When he had finished, he pulled me down the hill to the driveway so that I could look up and get the full effect. He was very proud.

Ah. . . yes. It was quite a view from below. Perched on the fence, leaning against the house for balance, was a smallish figure. He was wearing a grey sweatshirt, navy sweatpants, and old tennis shoes. His head was the tether ball, long ago stuffed away in the toolshed after the rope broke, gently discoloring and deflating over the years of banishment among the cobwebs. Upon his head perched a bright red baseball cap. The hands were stuffed mittens. It was an impressive little person indeed.

What my little son did not realize was that he had spent the afternoon recreating his brother. The clothes were mostly Adam's, and the baseball cap especially had become a kind of symbol for Adam's fight with cancer as it covered his bald little head—a head as bald and round as a tether ball. No, Luke was unaware of what he had done, but the rest of us all drew in our breath every time we drove into the driveway and looked up at that drooping yet somehow stalwart little figure resting against his home, waiting at the gate for us.

Unconsciously, Luke had valiantly worked at resurrection. And this is what we all do, or try to do, in the face of great loss. Tim O'Brien wanted to "save Linda's life" by writing about her. "In a story," he writes, "I can revive, at least briefly, that which is absolute and unchanging. . . . Linda can smile and sit up. She can reach out and say, "Timmy, stop crying."

In the face of death, we wonder how we can fill the gaping hole before us. How can we make old things new again? We may try, but we will not be satisfied. We can revive a bit through a story or a summer afternoon's labor of love, but all our resurrections this side of heaven begin with a lower case "r." Only the "upper case Resurrection," the Easter Resurrection, can deliver what we really want. In the meantime, we can (and should!), as the poet Wendell

Berry suggests, "practice resurrection." How do we do that? Here are a few suggestions from Berry's poem on the subject:

> Love the Lord, Love the world.
>
> Love someone who does not deserve it.
>
> Ask the questions that have no answers.
>
> Be joyful though you have considered all the facts.[2]

We must be very careful with how we go about living this glorious, fragile gift of life. And, if we are an Easter people, we must trust and proclaim that death does not get the last laugh. We do—because of Jesus.

> Where, O death, is your victory? Where, O death, is your sting? (1 Corinthians 15:55, NIV)

---

2. Berry, "Manifesto," 17

Heart's Desire

I think the sun is a flower
that blooms for just one hour. . .[1]

—RAY BRADBURY, "ALL SUMMER IN A DAY"

This is probably my favorite short story by the remarkable science fiction writer Ray Bradbury. It centers around a group of children who live on the planet Venus. All of the children have only known Venus as home, with the exception of Margot, who lived for a few years on planet Earth before her parents joined this expedition. The planet Venus is so different from the planet Earth. It rains constantly on Venus—Bradbury calls it "a concussion of storms"—which results in lots of vegetation, and the unrelenting weather keeps everyone trapped inside. However, once every seven years, for just two hours, the sun comes out on Venus. And as the story begins, the children are eagerly anticipating the arrival of this thing called "Sun." Margot writes a poem about it, comparing the sun to a flower that "blooms for just one hour." She can hardly wait because there is a small part of her that has a vague *remembrance* of the welcome warmth of the sun, even though she was very small when her parents took her to Venus. She has a sense of it and an intense desire to see it again. The children are eager, but Margot is craving.

There is a wonderful word for the desire she feels, a word that is not used much anymore. Margot is *yearning* for the sun. I once asked the students in my Old Testament class what they thought was the difference between *wishing* and *yearning*. According to them, wishing is more superficial—you wish for a certain Christmas gift or to go to Disney World, while yearning goes deeper—you yearn for a return to innocence or for someone you lost to come back.

1. Bradbury, "All Summer in a Day", 103.

According to Dr. Cornelius Plantinga, yearning is "part of the soul's standard equipment."[2] In other words, when God created us, he instilled in each one of us a desire for something that gets at the essence of who we are and why we are here. And what is that longing? It is to find our connection with God, it is to dwell in that "far off country" which awaits us after death, it is the promise of real glory. C.S. Lewis calls this yearning the "truest index" of reality.[3]

Yet we are almost embarrassed to speak of it. Perhaps that is because the yearning goes so deep. The Bible is full of imagery of what this "far off country" is like—death is swallowed up, all tears are wiped away, a room has been prepared in a mansion, a garden city is filled with all the glories of the nations, a river of life flows, the tree of life grows, and God's glory makes the sun unnecessary. All of these images (and many more) are meant to beckon us, to awaken us to what is waiting for those who dare to hope and believe that our strongest yearnings will be answered with God's final "yes!"

> He who was seated on the throne said, "I am making everything new." (Revelation 21:5, NIV)

2. Plantinga, *Engaging God's World*, 6.
3. Lewis, *The Weight of Glory and Other Addresses*, 15.

Wisdom

What God Is

"Did you ever talk to Dr. Hoenikker?" I asked Miss Faust.

"Oh, certainly. I talked to him a lot."

"Do any conversations stick in your mind?"

"There was one where he bet I couldn't tell him anything that was absolutely true. So I said to him, 'God is love.'"

"And what did he say?"

"He said, 'What is God? What is love?'"

"Um."

"But God really *is* love, you know," said Miss Faust, "no matter what Dr. Hoenikker said."[1]

—KURT VONNEGUT, *CAT'S CRADLE*

In *A Man Without a Country*, American author Kurt Vonnegut writes, "If I should ever die, God forbid, I hope you will say, 'Kurt is up in heaven now.' That's my favorite joke."[2] Sadly, Vonnegut died in 2007, yet his Twitter account, which tweets out one of his quotes daily, sent this one out just the other day. It saddened me. So it goes.

I've read most of Vonnegut's work. I love it. It's sarcastic and satirical and funny. He's critical of politicians, social norms, and very often religion. The focus of his religious criticism often centers on the idea that God is a fairy tale—similar to Santa Claus or the Tooth Fairy—and that adult human beings should be smart enough to know better. The dialogue from *Cat's Cradle* between Miss Faust and Dr. Hoenikker implies as much.

1. Vonnegut, *Cat's Cradle*, 54-55.
2. Vonnegut, *A Man Without A Country*, 80.

I have a feeling, however, that I read this passage differently than Vonnegut intended. In my opinion, Miss Faust's answer to Dr. Hoenikker was perfect: God is love. And that *is* an absolute truth. And I find her childlike faith, although it's probably meant to look foolish and naive, endearing. Her insistence at the end of the conversation is assured, and I like her more for it.

But this passage also ends the chapter. We learn of no further dialogue between the two on this topic. And *that* is disconcerting. Although we are called to have a childlike faith, it's also nice to be able to speak up to the Dr. Hoenikkers of the world and offer reason for his existence. I'm not sure what I would have said to Dr. Hoenikker in that exact moment. Perhaps I'd have clammed up as Miss Faust did, but given some time and another opportunity, I might have responded to the science-focused doctor with the testimony of a man far more intelligent than myself: C.S. Lewis. Lewis wasn't always sure of his own faith, but it was reason that made him the great theologian we know today. In *Mere Christianity*, Lewis explains, "If I find in myself a desire which no experience in this world can satisfy, the most probable explanation is that I was made for another world."[3]

What Lewis is describing is actually a very scientific approach to faith. In the early fourteenth century, William of Occam proposed the scientific principle today known as Occam's Razor. Simply put, he claimed that the hypothesis with the fewest assumptions should be the one selected as true. William of Occam himself was a Christian, and St. Thomas Aquinas and others applied his theory to belief in God. They argue that when there are no simpler answers for all of life's mysteries and miracles, the simplest and most profound explanation must be God. It's a beautifully logical approach to faith. And it's one that C.S. Lewis again, sums up beautifully: "I gave in, and admitted that God was God." And that's the truth. . . no matter what Dr. Hoenikker says.

> Truly I tell you, anyone who will not receive the kingdom of God like a little child will never enter it. (Mark 10:15, NIV)

3. Lewis, *Mere Christianity*, 136–37.

Time Optimists

> . . . But all people at root are time optimists. We all think
> there's enough time to do things with other people. Time to
> say things to them. And then something happens and we
> stand there holding on to words like "if."[1]

—FREDRIK BACKMAN, *A MAN CALLED OVE*

A Man Called Ove is a feel-good book about an unlikely subject.
The main character, Ove, is an aging curmudgeon who, having lost
his wife, no longer wants to continue living his own life. However,
his neighbors, acquaintances, and even a *cat* somehow thwart his
plans to give up on life. The lines above are the omniscient narrator
commenting on how people are always surprised when someone
they had assumed would always be there suddenly disappears.
Somehow we always think we have enough time to follow through
on plans or say the things we ought to say.

And then we are left with that little word "if"—if I had just
paid some attention to that girl who changed schools because she
couldn't find community here, if only I had been more careful with
what I said to the guy who used to be my best friend, if I had just
visited my grandma when she asked me to, if only I hadn't left
the house so angry that morning. . . . If—just two letters long, but
potentially devastating.

A former student told me that she chose *A Man Called Ove*
for a paper and presentation in a college psychology class. At
the end of her presentation, there was time given for comment
or questions. The overwhelming responses, she said, felt a bit like
a group therapy session. In particular, the "time optimist" quote
triggered many expressions of regret. One person's story touched
her deeply. He spoke of how he and his sister had never gotten

1. Backman, *A Man Called Ove*, 325.

along very well—they were so politically different, and they had been very competitive growing up. After years of silence, observing two siblings thoroughly enjoying each other's company one day made him decide to call his sister, who lived in another state, to apologize. They had a wonderful, healing conversation, and both agreed to call once per week from then on. However, it was a short-lived plan, since two months later the sister was killed in a terrible accident. He finished his story by saying, "I just keep thinking about how *grateful* I am that I swallowed my pride and made that connection. And what had kept us apart all those years was, in retrospect, so petty. If we had come to our senses sooner we could have been there for each other."

Eventually, Ove comes to terms with his regrets over his wife's death. When he lets go of some of his pain and anger, he begins to allow other people into his life. His bitterness recedes, and he is a better man. No one lives a regret-free life. If it is too late to repair whatever damage you have done in a relationship, look for ways you can use your regret to make better choices in the future. And if it is not too late for repair—get going! Who knows how much time you still have to swallow your pride or anger or bitterness or fear, allowing a healing delight in the freedom of hope and forgiveness?

> Teach us to number our days, that we may gain a heart of wisdom. (Psalm 90:12, NIV)

Small, Good Things

> And now for your blunders. You first of all allowed the pa-
> tient to read a book he really enjoyed because he enjoyed
> it and not in order to make clever remarks about it to his
> new friends. In the second place, you allowed him to walk
> down to the old mill and have tea there—a walk through
> country he really likes, and taken alone. In other words
> you allowed him two real positive Pleasures. Were you so
> ignorant as not to see the danger of this?[1]
>
> —C. S. Lewis, *The Screwtape Letters*

C.S. Lewis wrote *The Screwtape Letters* because he thought that
people in the modern world were not taking the devil seriously.
It is, as the title indicates, a series of letters written by a "higher
demon" named Screwtape to his nephew Wormwood, a novice
demon. Wormwood has been given the task of securing the dam-
nation of the soul of a young man.

And he's not very good at it. He goes for the obvious things,
like making the man afraid or angry or impatient with his mother.
All very well, says Screwtape, but more souls are won through
subtlety than through outright attack. The passage above is an
example of that. *Pleasure* is a God thing. The best the devil can
do in regard to pleasure is to *warp* it. So laughter, which is one of
God's most delightful gifts, in the devil's hands becomes a twisted
form of laughter, like mockery, or a dirty joke. Or the pleasure of
sex—God's idea originally—becomes warped by lust, which is really sex without the intimacy of relationship first. An important
truth about the devil is that unlike God, he cannot create. He can
only twist and warp what God has created.

---

1. Lewis, *The Screwtape Letters*, 58.

The "blunder" that Screwtape criticizes Wormwood for here is that Wormwood allowed his assigned human simple, positive pleasures. One was reading a good book. The other was enjoying a leisurely walk and a cup of tea. Small, good things. How could a demon warp these pure pleasures? I leave it to you to think of the possibilities.

Life's pleasures—the *genuine* pleasures, both large and small, are meant to do two things for us. First, God created them to delight us, for this is what the lover always intends for the beloved. When we give someone we truly love a gift, we choose it with care, and we are so eager to see the reaction it brings. And second, God created pleasure in the hope that we would acknowledge *him* as the giver. What a tragedy to simply receive and fail to say thank you! Our thanks, therefore, gives *him* pleasure, which should be of great importance to us.

This is a true story. One day a few summers ago I was sitting on our front porch in the early morning, beginning my day with devotions, as is my habit. I was praying with my eyes open, and suddenly a tiny, brilliantly colored goldfinch landed on the sill of the porch inches away from me. I caught my breath and whispered, "Thank You, God, for the color yellow." The bird flew off, but within seconds *two* goldfinches landed almost as close. It felt like God was whispering back, "So you liked that? Let me give you double!" That's the way God is.

Screwtape warns Wormwood, "Nothing matters at all except the tendency of a given state of mind, in given circumstances, to move a particular person at a particular moment nearer to God or nearer to us."[2] Every time we delight in small, good things, we push back the powers of darkness.

> You have made known to me the path of life; you will fill me with joy in your presence, with eternal pleasures at your right hand. (Psalm 16:11, NIV)

---

2. Lewis, *The Screwtape Letters*, 87–88.

Greater Complexities

> Obierika was a man who had thought about things. When
> the will of the goddess had been done, he sat down in his
> *obi* and mourned his friend's calamity. Why should a man
> suffer so grievously for an offense he had committed inad-
> vertently? But although he thought for a long time he found
> no answer. He was merely led into greater complexities.[1]
>
> —CHINUA ACHEBE, *THINGS FALL APART*

In Achebe's great novel *Things Fall Apart*, the main character,
Okonkwo, is banished for accidentally committing a crime. His
gun explodes, and the shrapnel takes a young man's life. The in-
cident was accidental and unavoidable, yet according to the clan's
laws, Okonkwo loses his home, relinquishes his titles, and is sent
to live in another land for seven years. For Okonkwo, this punishment is akin to taking his life. All he had worked hard to achieve
is gone in an instant. He accepts the banishment without question. But to Obierika, Okonkwo's best friend, it doesn't seem fair.
Obierika begins asking questions about the tribe's justice system,
their rituals, and their gods.

Questions are normal. We all ask them. Already, as young-
sters, we ask about Bible stories—which are meant to be taken
literally, and which aren't? We ask about theology—how can God
be Father, Son, and Holy Spirit, three in one? We have questions
about God's involvement in our world—how can bad things happen to good people? And we have questions about salvation and
life after death—who is saved and how can we be sure?

Like the questions Obierika asks in Achebe's novel, these
questions don't always come with clear answers. Often, in asking them, we are "led into greater complexities." For some, this

---

1. Achebe, *Things Fall Apart*, 125.

becomes problematic. When the questions asked don't come with clear answers, it can be a sticking point. For many, a lack of answers leads to a lack of faith. In the google-everything world we live in, we're used to having every answer at the touch of a keyboard, but some answers aren't available from a search engine. Christ calls us to a childlike faith, but that can be easier said than done. Yet, we sometimes have to acknowledge that we don't (and won't) know everything.

In *Things Fall Apart*, Obierika is characterized as the wisest character in the novel—and much of that might be attributed to his willingness to ask questions, even ones he can't come up with answers to. As Christians, we can and must be willing to do likewise. It is okay to live in the unknowing. In fact, it's necessary. Theologian Richard Rohr explains, "People who've had any genuine spiritual experience always know that they don't know. They are utterly humbled before mystery. They are in awe before the abyss of it all, in wonder at eternity and depth, and a Love, which is incomprehensible to the mind."[2]

> Do not be anxious about anything, but in every situation, by prayer and petition, with thanksgiving, present your requests to God. And the peace of God, which transcends all understanding, will guard your hearts and your minds in Christ Jesus. (Philippians 4:6–7, NIV)

---

2. Rohr, "Utterly Humbled by Mystery."

Who's Boss Here?

"Who's boss here?"

"I am," said Ralph loudly.

A little boy who wore the remains of an extraordinary black cap on his red hair and who carried the remains of a pair of spectacles at his waist, started forward, then changed his mind and stood still.[1]

—WILLIAM GOLDING, *LORD OF THE FLIES*

I went to Immanuel Christian, a small private Christian school, from kindergarten through twelfth grade. Academically, the school was top notch. Our sports teams always competed strongly, and the community there was wonderful. I was proud to be an Immanuel Eagle. . . most of the time. In high school, when my social life began to expand beyond the confines of the Immanuel Christian community, I wasn't always eager to share where I attended classes. I was always anxious about the questions that would follow: "A Christian school?" "Do you just learn about the Bible?" "Why do you go there?"

As a teenager, these weren't conversations I was excited to be a part of. I was a Christian. I was proud to be a Christian. I just wasn't always willing to accept the responsibility of being a Christian.

The ending of William Golding's *Lord of the Flies* always gets me thinking of those high school days. The parallel isn't exact—I wasn't a choir boy, never killed a pig for sport, and haven't been marooned on an island where I quickly and brutally descended into savagery—but there is one scene that resonates with me. When the boys are discovered at the end of the novel, the naval

---

1. Golding, *Lord of the Flies*, 201.

officer asks the boys who was in charge. Throughout the novel, both Ralph and Jack assert their leadership. Ralph is chosen as leader early, but throughout the novel, Jack works to usurp that power. He insists he is right for the job and does whatever is necessary to show he can be head honcho. He wants the responsibility of leadership when surrounded by his peers, but when it comes time to take responsibility for that role to a new audience, he shrinks away. Golding describes him as "a little boy" who "started forward, then changed his mind and stood still."

The scene reminds me of those high school conversations. In school, at home, and at church, I was proud to announce my love for the Lord. But when the same opportunities arose and responding confidently as a Christian would come with some consequences (as small as they may be), I wasn't as eager to speak up. Like Jack, when asked to stand up and take responsibility, I too often "stood still."

Today, I look back and regret the missed opportunities. I blew it. I hope I've grown from them, and I have confidence today I didn't have then. As a Christian, it's important that I do. Jack fails to take ownership and responsibility after he is saved. For Christians, taking ownership and responsibility of our calling should happen *because* we are saved.

> Whoever acknowledges me before others, I will also acknowledge before my Father in heaven. But whoever disowns me before others, I will disown before my Father in heaven. (Matthew 10:32–33, NIV)

Finding Your Voice

First thing she had to remember was she was not at home.
. . . She had to let them know how she and Tea Cake had
been with one another. . . . She tried to make them see how
she couldn't ever want to be rid of him. She didn't plead
to anybody. She just sat there and told and when she was
through she hushed.[1]

—ZORA NEALE HURSTON, *THEIR EYES WERE WATCHING GOD*

Janie, the stunningly beautiful heroine of this novel, finally finds
love on the third try. His nickname is "Tea Cake." She struggles
through abuse and misunderstanding with two other men before
him, but finally she meets her soulmate. He makes her laugh. He
respects her opinions. He admonishes her gently and praises her
lavishly. He even gives up his life protecting her. And now, ironically, Janie is on trial for his murder.

Throughout the novel, Janie is trying to find her own voice.
That may sound like a strange quest, but in truth, it is a universal
one. From the time we speak our first words, we begin to grasp
how powerful language can be. It is the way we get what we want
or need. It is the way we protest. It is the way we find answers to
our questions. It is the way we speak what is in our heart. At the
beginning of her life, Janie is too afraid and weak to have much of
a voice—all her objections are easily dismissed because she can
never argue her own side effectively. Later, she finds a strong, stri-
dent voice, but it is often cruel and careless. But Tea Cake shows
her how to speak her mind and heart *gracefully*.

When Janie is put on trial, she is given the opportunity to
defend herself. There are four important things she uses as tools to
do so. *First, she pauses and reminds herself of where she is.* This is a

1. Hurston, *Their Eyes Were Watching God,* 187.

good thing for all of us to remember when we are about to speak. What is appropriate for this particular audience? What should they hear from us? What *shouldn't* they hear? *Second, she tries to make them understand.* She paints them a picture of herself and the man she loved. Again, this is a wise move. Allowing emotional outbursts to overtake a careful choice of words generally leads to a defensive or negative response from those we may be trying to persuade or convince. Let the picture you paint speak for itself. *Third, she doesn't beg or plead for the outcome she desires.* In doing so, she gives her audience room to think rationally. She lets the air move. *And finally, "when she was through, she hushed."* Too many words weaken the power of a few well-chosen ones. The queen's line "Methinks the lady doth protest too much" from Shakespeare's *Hamlet* comes to mind.[2]

The book of Proverbs is full of advice about the effective use of voice. Rather than close this particular devotional with just one verse, I'll challenge you to take a moment and ponder how Janie's calculated use of voice is really a biblical concept set forth over and over again in this wise book of pithy sayings.

> The wise in heart are called discerning, and pleasant words promote instruction. (Proverbs 16:21, NIV)

> Pleasant words are a honeycomb, sweet to the soul and healing to the bones. (Proverbs 16:24, NIV)

> Avoid a man who talks too much. (Proverbs 19:20b, NIV)

> The tongue that brings healing is a tree of life, but a deceitful tongue crushes the spirit. (Proverbs 15:4, NIV)

> Lips that speak knowledge are a rare jewel. (Proverbs 20:15b, NIV)

> He who speaks before listening—that is his folly and his shame. (Proverbs 18:13, NIV)

2. Shakespeare, *Hamlet*, 151.

A gentle answer turns away wrath, but a harsh word stirs up anger. (Proverbs 15:1, NIV)

When words are many, sin is not absent, but he who knows when to hold his tongue is wise. (Proverbs 10:19, NIV)

Reckless words pierce like a sword, but the tongue of the wise brings healing. (Proverbs 12:18, NIV)

A wise man's heart guides his mouth and his lips promote instruction. (Proverbs 16:23, NIV)

Which Way to Jump, or Fall

And then when the startled dust had settled down about Montag's mind, Faber began, softly, "All right, he's had his say. You must take it in. I'll say my say, too, in the next few hours. And you'll take it in. And you'll try to judge them and make your decision as to which way to jump, or fall. But I want it to be your decision, not mine, and not the Captain's. But remember that the Captain belongs to the most dangerous enemy of truth and freedom, the solid unmoving cattle of the majority. Oh, God, the terrible tyranny of the majority. We all have our harps to play. And it's up to you now to know with which ear you'll listen."[1]

—RAY BRADBURY, *FAHRENHEIT 451*

Guy Montag is a fireman. He's not a fireman as we know them today—he starts fires. Montag burns books which, in Bradbury's classic *Fahrenheit 451*, are the greatest threat to humanity. Books cause citizens to think, to question, to look for meaning beyond the television screens in their parlors. Yet early in the novel, Guy brings a book home.

Beatty is the fire chief. He's "the bad guy" in the novel. He enforces the destruction of books (although it's clear from his dialogue he's well-read himself), and he indoctrinates his firemen as to why their job is so necessary. In a way, he's like a small, animated devil standing on Montag's shoulder, constantly telling him to do what we, the readers, know is terrible.

Which makes Faber the angel on Montag's shoulder. Montag hears Faber's voice (literally, as he wears an earpiece connected to Faber's radio) talking sense into the situation, explaining to him what we, the readers, feel Montag *should* do. Faber encourages

1. Bradbury, *Fahrenheit 451*, 104.

Montag to go against "the terrible tyranny of the majority." He wants Montag to question his role in this world of constant entertainment and unfulfillment. Faber values literature and learning. He represents Bradbury's perspective, and when he criticizes the "solid unmoving cattle of the majority," it is a commentary on the way our society is evolving. There are lessons to be learned from *Fahrenheit 451*. It's a book worth reading, not burning.

But what I find most important in the passage above is how Faber does not simply force his alternate perspective on Montag. He will give his thoughts, but he challenges Montag to make up his own mind. Rather than simply replacing Beatty as the message controlling Montag's thought processes, he challenges Montag to "try to judge them and make [his] decision as to which way to jump, or fall." When push comes to shove, Faber makes it clear—what Montag chooses is up to Montag.

Following Christ works in much the same way. Often challenging Christians to act contrary to the "solid unmoving cattle of the majority" that is our world, the life of Christ in the New Testament gives us a vision of how we *should* live our lives. But our all-powerful, almighty God still leaves things up to us. It's amazing really. Rather than creating us as mindless servants, following without purpose or question, the Lord designed us with wisdom and the ability to discern what is his will. He gives us the choice. The decisions we make are our own.

But too often we make the wrong decisions. We do things that hurt others, we make selfish choices, or we reject God's call entirely. Sin can offer many convincing and tempting alternatives to God's plan every moment of the day. Yet God tasks us with the responsibility to choose how we'll respond. We need to decide which way to jump, or fall.

There are always going to be contrasting messages buzzing in our ears. "And it's up to you now to know with which ear you will listen."

> Do not quench the Spirit. Do not treat prophecies with contempt but test them all; hold on to what is good, reject every kind of evil. (1 Thessalonians 5:19–22, NIV)

Going Further into the Matter

> It was Dr. Ransom who first saw that our only chance was to publish in the form of *fiction* what would certainly not be listened to as fact. He even thought—greatly overrating my literary powers—that this might have the incidental advantage of reaching a wider public, and that, certainly, it would reach a great many people sooner than "Weston." To my objection that if accepted as fiction it would for that reason be regarded as false, he replied that there would be indications enough in the narrative for the few readers—the very few—who at *present* were prepared to go further into the matter.[1]
>
> —C. S. Lewis, *Out of the Silent Planet*

Ethos, pathos, and logos: these are Aristotle's modes of persuasion, or the building blocks to a good argument. I teach these three Greek terms to my speech classes, I encourage their use in my writing classes, and I challenge my speech team to consider them as well. They know these three terms well by the time they leave my classroom.

Ethos is easy for them to understand. It's all about them after all—it relates to the speakers or writers and the credibility they bring to the argument being presented. Do they look prepared when they step up in front of the classroom? Did they dress up for a speech tournament?

They also quickly see the importance of logos. Logos, or the necessity for logic or reasoning, feels most schoolish. Using research they've collected, whether it be facts or stats or quotations, feels necessary for the essays and speeches they're crafting.

---

1. Lewis, *Out of the Silent Planet*, 152.

Every addition to the works cited list seems like it's one step closer to an A+.

But students don't always see the value in pathos. Convincing them to add a story, personal or otherwise, as a means of connecting to their audience isn't easy. They often feel it's a waste of time.

As an English teacher, however, I know the value of a story; it's the impetus for this devotional book. Harper Lee's *To Kill a Mockingbird* teaches empathy and courage far better than any lecture could, and Aldous Huxley's *Brave New World* can shock students into thinking twice about the media they consume daily better than continued warnings from their parents. When delivered more directly, messages are often rejected quickly because many of us don't want to be told what to believe or do. A story can bring us to truths more effectively.

C.S. Lewis also understands the importance of pathos. Although he wrote a lot of nonfiction, much of his energy was also dedicated to crafting stories. The novels of Narnia, letters between Screwtape and Wormwood, and his science fiction trilogy all seem to demonstrate what Dr. Ransom says in the quote above—that fiction "might have the incidental advantage of reaching a wider public."

And, of course, Jesus's parables in the Gospels have the same effect. Preaching forgiveness may not have sunk in as deeply as his stories about the prodigal son or the two debtors. Lost sheep and lost coins may connect more quickly to someone who can't understand how they can be loved by an all-powerful God. And the Kingdom of Heaven is tough to comprehend, but an agricultural society easily understood sowing and mustard seeds.

There is, of course, a danger: some may hear the stories and leave them as simply that—stories. But, in the stories of Lewis, the parables of Christ, the novels that are quoted in this book, and the texts in my English classes, there are "indications enough in the narrative[s] for the few readers. . . who at *present* were prepared to go further into the matter."

> The disciples came to him and asked, "Why do you speak
> to the people in parables?"

He replied, "Because the knowledge of the secrets of the kingdom of heaven has been given to you, but not to them. Whoever has will be given more, and they will have an abundance. Whoever does not have, even what they have will be taken from them. This is why I speak to them in parables:

'Though seeing, they do not see;
though hearing, they do not hear or understand.'"
(Matthew 13:10–13, NIV)

Purpose

The Big Question

What'll we do with ourselves this afternoon, and the day
after that, and the next thirty years?[1]

—F. Scott Fitzgerald, *The Great Gatsby*

Daisy asks this question as she lounges in her extravagant home
along with her friend Jordan; her husband, Tom; and her lover,
Gatsby. The four of them are languishing in the heat of the day and
the extravagance of their empty lives. It is a question the modern
world asks; the world of our ancestors did not have time to ask it.
As life became easier with modern conveniences, and as wealth
afforded more time for play, the tedium and semi-desperation of
eking out a living loosened its grip a bit on most people, affording
them the luxury of "free time." Ironically, many of us don't always
know what to do with it.

Think of it this way. School lets out for summer. The initial
burst of freedom is exhilarating, and the world seems full of possibility. But day follows day, and as the newness of free time wears a
bit thin, we oddly feel at a loss, and almost—almost!— wish for the
routine of school, with its tiny pockets of freedom amidst the rigor
of required work. Somehow, small doses seem tastier than the open
spaces of days where we are, frankly, bored.

Time is a gift that is given to each of us. Some get a little; some
get a lot. Regardless, we are asked to use it responsibly. What does
that look like? The reason Daisy asks her whining question is that
her life lacks any purpose or meaning beyond the self-serving,
spoiled lifestyle she has grown accustomed to. When we speak of
someone living a full life, it does not necessarily mean "full of years."
It is more likely that we are referring to a life that has been filled
up and then poured out with the quest for knowledge, meaningful
relationships, and living for something bigger than self.

1. Fitzgerald, *The Great Gatsby*, 118.

I once had a small poster on the podium in my classroom that said: "Complacency destroys body, mind, spirit." At the end of the semester, one of my students stayed after class for a moment to ask me about it. He said, "You know, I've looked at that sign almost every day, and I keep wondering, what does *complacency* mean?" I smiled and said, in typical English teacher fashion, "Well, why don't you look it up and find out?" His response says it all: "Naw. . . I don't really care that much."

> The sluggard buries his hand in the dish; he is too lazy to bring it back to his mouth. (Proverbs 26:15, NIV)

Fault

> [Bernard] was as miserably isolated now as he had been
> when the service began—more isolated by reason of his
> unreplenished emptiness, his dead satiety. . . . He had
> emerged from that crimson twilight into the common
> electric glare with a self-consciousness intensified to the
> pitch of agony. He was utterly miserable, and perhaps, per-
> haps it was his own fault.[1]
>
> —ALDOUS HUXLEY, *BRAVE NEW WORLD*

Every semester, as I begin to teach Aldous Huxley's classic novel
Brave New World, I worry. The novel tackles big issues in shocking and provocative ways: sex, drugs, cloning, suicide, and a sharp
criticism of the church. I worry there will be a phone call from an
angry parent, grandparent, or principal. I worry students will be
too offended. I worry they won't be offended at all. But, regardless
of all my worries, I consistently come back to the same conclusion:
it's a text that needs to be taught.

Huxley's New World sparks classroom discussions about class
systems, government structures, and our consumerist culture. The
first four chapters prompt mini-lessons and conversations about
communism, Freud, and indoctrination—and my students are
quick to side with Huxley and his comments about our world.
Then, chapter five happens.

Major character Bernard Marx attends a worship service.
Those in attendance sing songs, share in a litany, and have their
own form of communion. Although Huxley pushes the boundar-
ies in his critique when it comes to depicting church fellowship
(members conclude the service with a drug-induced orgy), what is
truly disheartening is the main character's response to the service:

---

1. Huxley, *Brave New World*, 86.

"[Bernard] was as miserably isolated now as he had been when the service began. . . and perhaps, perhaps it was his own fault."

I often ask my students if they've ever felt the same way. Has church ever made them feel less loved, less connected, and less happy than before they went? They often, sometimes reluctantly, admit it's true. Then we discuss why this might be the case.

Sometimes the church doesn't do what the church is called to do. Sometimes people feel disconnected where they should feel loved. Sometimes things are said or not said that make people feel excluded. Sometimes the people there aren't as welcoming as they should be. And in each of these instances, we are called as Christians to make the church a better place. But sometimes, as Bernard admits after leaving the service, the church has done all it can. And then, it's my students I begin to worry about.

> I pray that the eyes of your heart may be enlightened in order that you may know the hope to which he has called you, the riches of his glorious inheritance in his holy people, and his incomparably great power for us who believe. (Ephesians 1:18–19, NIV)

Lighting Little Fires Everywhere
and Anywhere

> "Well?" said Mia, "What are you going to do about it?"
>
> It was not a question Izzy had been asked before. Until now her life had been one of mute, futile fury. . . . What was she going to do about it? The very idea that she *could* do something stunned her.[1]
>
> —Celeste Ng, *Little Fires Everywhere*

There is a character in C.S. Lewis' book *The Great Divorce* who is particularly intriguing because he is cynical about absolutely everything. When the narrator of the story asks him what Peking was like, he responds, "Nothing to it. Just one darn wall inside another. Just a trap for tourists. I've been pretty well everywhere, Niagara Falls, the Pyramids, Salt Lake City, the Taj Mahal. . . . Not worth looking at. All advertisement stunts." Both characters have just arrived by bus from hell. When the narrator asks what he thought of it there, he says: "Yes—that's a flop too. They lead you to expect red fire and devils and all sorts of interesting people sizzling on grids. . . but when you get there, it's just like any other town."[2]

What ensues is a conversation where the cynic waxes eloquent on pretty much everything that is wrong with the world, and when he finally stops to take a breath, the narrator asks him a really important question: "What would you like to do if you had your choice?" *And the cynic has no answer.* He basically asserts that he can only point out what's wrong—making things right again is not his job.

In the book *Little Fires Everywhere*, Izzy has a similar attitude. Unlike her siblings, who unquestioningly accept a life of

1. Ng, *Little Fires Everywhere*, 79.
2. Lewis, *The Great Divorce*, 52-53.

privilege and don't think much beyond school activities, looking fashionable, or hanging out with the right people, Izzy finds her family boring and hypocritical. And she's pretty much right. The problem is that she's a masterful critic who sits in judgment, so to speak, with her hands folded in her lap. When Mia, the house-keeper, asks her what course of action she could take to make things better, she is stunned.

Gandhi's famous quote: "Be the change you want to see in the world" gets to the heart of this.[3] It takes courage to do this. A recent example that has sparked huge controversy involves the San Francisco 49ers quarterback Colin Kaepernick, who protest-ed the lack of "liberty and justice for all" Americans by kneeling during the National Anthem. He said, "I am not going to stand up to show pride in a flag for a country that oppresses black people and people of color."[4] Think what you like about this action, but this young man put his convictions out front. He even donated $1 million of his own salary to several organizations that are invest-ed in causes of social justice. After hearing his nationally televised interview, the 49ers also pledged $1 million to two organizations working against racism.

Ah, but what can people with little power or influence do? The world is such a mess. The answer: do what you can in your small corner of the world. Recently, several high school students, upon learning details about the plight of displaced families in Syria (nearly half the population!), decided to use their talents to create beautiful handmade stationery sets and sell them to raise money for Preemp-tive Love Coalition, a non-profit organization which helps Syrians rebuild their lives. One small, inspiring example.

American writer and clergyman Edward Everett Hale once wrote: "I am only one; but still I am one. I cannot do everything; but still I can do something."[5] We must not simply resort to shak-ing our collective heads and sighing our collective sighs and sitting with our collective hands in our laps. The world is crying out for

3. Gandhi, *Be the Change: A Grandfather Gandhi Story*, 5.

4. "Colin Kaepernick Explains Why He Sat During National Anthem."

5. *A Year of Beautiful Thoughts*, 172.

even small acts of mercy and love. What are we going to do about it? What are *you* going to do about it?

> Then I heard the voice of the Lord saying, "Whom shall I send? And who will go for us?" And I said, "Here am I. Send me!" (Isaiah 6:8, NIV)

Saying Equals Doing

> But language wasn't only for communication: it was also a
> form of action. According to speech act theory, statements
> like "You're under arrest," "I christen this vessel," or "I prom-
> ise" were all performative: a speaker could perform the
> action only by uttering the words. For such acts, knowing
> what would be said didn't change anything. Everyone at a
> wedding anticipated the words "I now pronounce you hus-
> band and wife," but until the minister actually said them,
> the ceremony didn't count. With performative language,
> saying equaled doing.[1]
>
> —Ted Chiang, "Story of Your Life"

My wife and I have, at times, taken classes offered through our
church to help strengthen our marriage. It's not that we were necessarily struggling (although there have been times of struggle),
but being married takes hard work and commitment. Marriage
classes have reminded us of that, and they have been very helpful
and healthy for us.

In one of these classes, the instructor spoke about how he,
when speaking to his wife, will often use the word "value" instead
of "love." "Love," he explained, is used casually or even flippantly too
often by nearly all of us. We're quick to blurt out "I love pizza!" or "I
loved that movie!" without a second thought, and therefore saying,
"I love you" to a spouse, he argued, didn't carry much weight. "Love"
is a word too often spoken to be particularly meaningful. Whereas
"value," he suggested, means something more. The word "value" implies a hierarchy of sorts—the things we *value* are things we would
not risk losing, we'd prioritize time for, and we'd work to maintain at

---

1. Chiang, "Story of Your Life", *Stories of Your Life and Others,* 138.

all costs. The instructor believed that saying "I value you" to his wife was more meaningful than "I love you."

Even though I am not entirely convinced of the importance of these particular semantics in my own marriage, I found it to be a great reminder of the importance of language when it comes to forming and maintaining relationships. I remember vividly (and not particularly fondly) an ex-girlfriend telling me she loved me, and me awkwardly thanking her rather than declaring my love in response. Needless to say, the relationship didn't last much longer. The word was more than a word in this instance; it was an action. "Saying equaled doing."

Ted Chiang's short story (and the basis for the film *Arrival*), "Story of Your Life," articulates this idea perfectly, calling it "performative language." In the short story, Chiang is writing about first contact with an alien species that Louise, the linguist contracted to speak to them, calls "heptapods." Chiang writes, "For the heptapods, all language was performative. Instead of using language to inform, they used language to actualize." Heptapods had knowledge of the future, so speaking something was unnecessary for communication, "but in order for their knowledge to be true, the conversation would have to take place."

The same could be said for prayer. God knows all of our needs, so speaking them to him isn't really necessary—yet it's required of us. I don't mean to imply that God doesn't do things for us without our request; however, God's knowledge of our thoughts and needs shouldn't minimize the importance of the request. Prayer is performative language in that it affirms the nature of our relationship with God. Much like saying "I love you" or "I value you" affirms my feelings for my wife (both for me as I say it, and her as she hears it), prayer reminds us of our reliance on God for all things: "Please God, heal my dad's cancer" affirms my need for God's power in my life. "Please God, forgive my dishonesty today at work" affirms my need for forgiveness and salvation. "God, thank you for the beautiful weather outside" solidifies my appreciation for all the blessings I receive. "I love you, Lord" is performative, just as when I say "I love my wife."

The next time you pray, consider your words carefully. They needn't be lofty or poetic, but when they are honest and precise and specific, they change the relationship you have with God. Saying equals doing.

> Is anyone among you suffering? Let him pray. Is anyone cheerful? Let him sing praise. Is anyone among you sick? Let him call for the elders of the church, and let them pray over him, anointing him with oil in the name of the Lord. And the prayer of faith will save the one who is sick, and the Lord will raise him up. And if he has committed sins, he will be forgiven. Therefore, confess your sins to one another and pray for one another, that you may be healed. (James 5:13–18, NIV)

To Wear an Identity

> And the character of Demosthenes gradually took on a life of his own. At times she found herself thinking like Demosthenes at the end of a writing session, agreeing with ideas that were supposed to be calculated poses. . . . Perhaps it's impossible to wear an identity without becoming what you pretend to be.[1]
>
> —ORSON SCOTT CARD, ENDER'S GAME

Orson Scott Card's *Ender's Game* has children taking on roles far beyond their years. The protagonist, Ender Wiggin, is earth's last hope for survival, and he must act as a leader in order to become one. He plays fighting simulation games for years, learning to orchestrate battle tactics, and in doing so, he becomes a brilliant tactician. Similarly, back on Earth, his brother and sister take on roles as political minds in online forums, challenging each other, and the world, to think about where things are going. Although much of what these preteens do is initially a façade, eventually their actions begin to define their true selves.

This applies to real life as well. In my freshman speech class, we watch a TED Talk titled, "Your Body Language May Shape Who You Are." In the video, Amy Cuddy explains how positive posture can increase one's confidence. She encourages her viewers to "fake it until [they] make it" and tells of her own transformation from a self-conscious and timid student to a successful teacher and speaker.[2] After watching this video, some of my students will strike "power poses" before their speeches.

This is also a lesson we can and should apply to our spiritual lives. Daily prayer, weekly church attendance, routine

---

1. Card, *Ender's Game*, 231.
2. Cuddy, "Your Body Language May Shape Who You Are."

devotionals, intentionally and routinely finding opportunities to serve: these things may feel forced at times, but the practice of them can change us. N.T. Wright, in *After You Believe: Why Christian Character Matters*, explains: "Virtue is what happens when someone has made a thousand small choices requiring effort and concentration to do something which is good and right, but which doesn't 'come naturally.' And then, on the thousand and first time, when it really matters, they find that they do what's required automatically."[3] Much like practicing a sport, focusing on living the Christian life comes with discipline.

And when we don't continue those practices, it's nearly impossible to remain devout. There's the temptation in our busy world to put aside faith practices—skipping church because Sundays are the only time to sleep in, quitting daily family devotions because someone has practice, or forgetting nightly prayers because it's been a long day—but we convince ourselves that we still *believe*, and that's what's important. But as theologian Jamie Smith writes, "When we try to think our way out of such inconsistencies, our behavior keeps coming back to bite us. That's because behavior is not driven by ideas. It is a bodily thing that reflects the way we order—or disorder—our loves and desires."[4] The body and mind can't be separated; one informs the other. Our actions change the way we think, feel, and believe, so focusing on those actions is key to our spiritual life.

When, in Card's novel, Valentine Wiggin takes on the persona of Demosthenes, everything she says is a ruse. She pretends to believe political ideas contrary to her own, but in typing up those thoughts, and in reading responses to her posts, she begins to believe in them. She comes to a conclusion that we, as Christians, can learn from and spin into a positive: "Perhaps it's impossible to wear an identity without becoming what you pretend to be." And perhaps wearing an identity—one marked by the Holy Spirit—is the way to become exactly what we are called to be.

---

3. Wright, *After You Believe*, 20.
4. Neff, "You Can't Think Your Way To God."

But someone will say, "You have faith, and I have works." Show me your faith without your works, and I will show you my faith by my works. (James 2:18, NIV)

Folks

> You never really understand a person until you consider things from his point of view. . . until you climb into his skin and walk around in it.[1]
>
> —HARPER LEE, *To Kill a Mockingbird*

This beautiful book, which won the Pulitzer Prize in 1961, is taught in almost every school in America. Interestingly, Harper Lee never really wrote another novel; *Go Set a Watchman*, published in 2015 but written in the mid 1950s, was really a first draft of *To Kill a Mockingbird*. Many people believe that *Mockingbird* was the story that burned in her soul and needed to be told, and after that she herself felt that she had nothing more to offer, or the pressure to produce another like it stifled her creativity and confidence. It is a worthy and eloquent contribution to the world, regardless.

Atticus is the one who gives his young daughter Scout the advice to walk in someone else's shoes. She is having difficulty getting along with people who criticize her father for his role in helping a black man get justice. His words highlight the difference between *sympathy* and *empathy*. Sympathy is a feeling of pity one feels for another person. It weeps from a distance. Empathy enlarges the scope to a shared understanding for that person. It enters in. A spectator watching a child try to hit the ball during a softball game may feel sympathy for his striking out time and again. Another spectator may watch the same event and go back in memory to his own terrible performance in softball as a child. Only the second spectator has walked in that child's shoes.

Later in the novel, when Jem tries to teach Scout what he thinks he has figured out about the categories of people in Maycomb (and the world), Scout responds with an innocent yet profound worldview of her own: "Naw, Jem. I think there's just one

1. Lee, *To Kill A Mockingbird*, 227

kind of folks. Folks."[2] My own experience as a leader in a prison book club has brought this truth home to me. Although I began this volunteer work to "give something back," I find that I always leave with new insight and a deepened respect for a community that is largely put away and forgotten by the rest of the world. Because of a terrible choice, a moment of passion, or a desperate attempt to change circumstances, these men now find themselves behind bars for life. And yet, these men, many of them who arrived in their twenties or younger and are now in their thirties and forties, are so much more than the one horrific crime that put them there. The book discussions are rich and insightful, and they never fail to do their assignments for the following week. But now, when I go to the beach and enjoy my kayak or a swim or simply lay in the sun, I remember them and grieve what has been taken from them. Things as simple as a cup of Starbucks coffee, sleeping in, a warm fire, a spontaneous evening out with my husband or a friend—these will more than likely never be a part of their experience again.

Is my response merely sympathy? I don't think so. And this is why: I have come to love these men. Their loss somehow both lessens and increases the pleasure of these things for me. I cannot simply say "too bad" because my heart has entered the picture. They have become "my folks." This is why Jem sobs at the outcome of Tom Robinson's trial, why Dill gets sick to his stomach when the prosecuting lawyer calls Tom "boy" over and over again, why Scout can take the arm of Boo Radley and escort him across the street to his home. To walk in someone's shoes is to tune your own heart to the melody of even the most unlikely of human beings and sing a mutual song with compassion.

> Rejoice with those who rejoice and mourn with those
> who mourn. (Romans 12:15, NIV)

2. Lee, *To Kill A Mockingbird*, 227.

Winners and Losers

"So, do you admire your father for surviving?"

"Well. . . sure, I know there was a lot of luck involved, but he was amazingly present-minded and resourceful. . . ."

"Then you think it's admirable to survive. Does that mean it's NOT admirable to NOT survive?"

"Whoosh. I-I think I see what you mean. It's as if life equals winning, so death equals losing."

"Yes, life always takes the side of life, and somehow the victims are blamed. But it wasn't the BEST people who survived, nor did the best ones die. It was RANDOM!"[1]

—ART SPIEGELMAN, *MAUS II: A SURVIVOR'S TALE: AND HERE MY TROUBLES BEGAN*

I love playing games. *Risk, Settlers of Catan, Ticket to Ride*, any form of card game—I've always loved the challenge of figuring out the best strategy to win. And I'm generally quite good at them. I like to think I win more often than I lose.

One game I never cared for growing up was *The Game of Life*. In the game, players spin a wheel, and the wheel tells how many spaces to move. Each space on the board dictates an event that happens in the player's life. These events include everything from graduation to career choice to marriage and children. Players don't get to choose what happens to them—it's assigned, at random. There is very little strategy or skill involved. The spin of the wheel is the determiner of success.

Although I never cared to play the game, I do think it's indicative of much of how the real game of life too often seems to work.

1. Spiegelman, *Maus II: A Survivor's Tale: And Here My Troubles Began*, 45.

We live in a world that tries to convince us that our hard work and decision-making lead to our success or failure in life. Wealth, power, success—we are taught that these are a result of how we *play* the game. And if we have the correct strategy or compete hard enough, we'll be winners. But, like *The Game of Life*, the reality is that things are often beyond our control.

Art Spiegelman's *Maus* series grapples with this issue in a scene from the second book where he discusses the Holocaust with his therapist. He struggles with the survival of his father, and how his father's life felt like winning, and that left Spiegelman feeling as if those who died at the hands of the Nazis seemed like losers. Spiegelman has trouble reconciling how any of what happened could make sense. Throughout the graphic novel, Spiegelman's father, Vladek, continually survived Nazi Germany by being in the right places at the right times. Although he did make some astute decisions along the way, Vladek wasn't the determiner of his survival, and his son recognizes this.

And although it isn't always the message we are presented with, our lives are much the same. Being born in the developed world as opposed to a third world country, inheriting an able mind and body rather than a mental or physical disability, having a supportive and healthy family versus a dysfunctional or abusive one: these are factors that no individual controls or can strategically avoid, but they definitely play a major role in whether or not people "win" in life.

Unlike *The Game of Life*, events in our life are not random. We have a creator who knows what was, what is, and what is to come. Oftentimes, we do not understand his plan—and for many who survived the Holocaust, this resulted in doubt in or rejection of God—but there is a plan. And the plan is not to pit humans in constant competition with each other.

For this reason, we need to constantly remind ourselves that winning, at least the way the world sees it, isn't the goal. Worldly successes aren't what we are aiming to achieve. Instead, we are called to love rather than compete. The life of Christ we are challenged to emulate was one of humility and service. And the true victory comes to us not through any skill or strategy, but through the grace of God.

> But many who are first will be last, and many who are last will be first. (Matthew 19:30, NIV)

Dangerous Folly

I have done no harm. But I remember now
I am in this earthly world; where to do harm
Is often laudable, to do good sometime
Accounted dangerous folly.[1]

—WILLIAM SHAKESPEARE, *MACBETH*

Terrorist attacks, natural disasters, and criminal trials: watching the nightly news can be tremendously despairing. We feel helpless and frustrated at injustice and despair around the world, so we change the channel to *Sportscenter* or *Entertainment Tonight*. And that's when things get *really* depressing.

A pop musician facing charges of domestic violence sells out a nation-wide tour. An actor nominated for an Oscar walks the red carpet smiling for photos while news breaks about their extra-marital affair with a co-star. A professional athlete makes racist remarks on social media one week and signs a multi-million dollar contract the next. Things don't seem right.

I think of this each time I teach Act IV of *Macbeth* to my students. Lady Macduff, in her lone scene in the play, sums up this frustration. As she is facing death, knowing she is completely in-nocent, she sadly exclaims, "I have done no harm," before offering her criticism of our world—we live in a world where those that do harm are often praised and doing good can be "dangerous folly." Again, things don't seem right.

And things aren't fair. The world is broken. Bad things often happen to good people. Children face hunger or homelessness be-fore they can possibly be expected to provide for themselves. Cancer comes to those who do everything possible to keep their bodies fit.

---

1. Shakespeare, *Macbeth*, 137.

Car accidents claim the safest of drivers. Sometimes, doing good feels like dangerous folly. But that shouldn't be a reason to stop.

In that fateful scene, Lady Macduff does not betray her husband. In the scenes that follow, her husband does not betray Scotland. And in the final scene of the play, Lady Macduff's words are shown to be inevitably untrue as good does prevail.

And it will in our world, too. And so, we continue doing good. We do it even when it doesn't seem to make a difference. We do it when others question or criticize us for it. And we do it with the knowledge that it will ultimately prevail. There's no folly in that.

> Let us now become weary in doing good, for at the proper time we will reap a harvest if we do not give up. (Galatians 6:9, NIV)

Losing Heart

[The overseer] Mr. Gore once undertook to whip one of
Colonel Lloyd's slaves, by the name of Demby. He had given
Demby but few stripes, when, to get rid of the scourging,
he ran and plunged himself into a creek and stood there at
the depth of his shoulders, refusing to come out. Mr. Gore
told him that he would give him three calls, and that, if he
did not come out at the third call, he would shoot him. The
first call was given. Demby made no response, but stood
his ground. The second and third calls were given with the
same result. Mr. Gore then, without consultation or delib-
eration with any one, not even giving Demby an additional
call, raised his musket to his face, taking deadly aim at his
standing victim, and in an instant poor Demby was no
more. His mangled body sank out of sight, and blood and
brains marked the water where he had stood.[1]

—FREDERICK DOUGLASS, *NARRATIVE OF THE LIFE
OF FREDERICK DOUGLASS*

The mass of men lead lives of quiet desperation.[2]

—HENRY DAVID THOREAU, *WALDEN*

Frederick Douglass is one of my heroes. He was born a slave,
not even aware of the date of his birth, and he did not grieve his
mother's death because he barely knew her. He was deprived of
an education because the slave masters believed (probably accu-
rately) that if their slaves learned, they would feel discontent and

1. Douglass, *Narrative of the Life of Frederick Douglass, an American
Slave,* 33.
2. Thoreau, *Walden,* 6.

try to flee. Somehow, Douglass managed to educate himself, and in the process, he miraculously became a powerful spokesperson for slaves both in America and in England.

Near the beginning of his autobiography, he tells us the story of Demby, one of the slaves of the wealthy and powerful Colonel Lloyd. Colonel Lloyd employed an overseer named Mr. Gore, who was, in Douglass's words "cruel enough to inflict the severest punishment, artful enough to descend to the lowest trickery, and obdurate enough to be insensible to the voice of a reproving conscience."[3] In other words: a sadist. He enjoyed the pain he inflicted and found the smallest excuse to torture these sad human beings who were placed, without their permission, under his control.

I think Douglass remembers Demby in particular because there was a point when he, like Demby, found himself standing at the edge of despair. For Douglass, it was years later under a man named Covey, who was nicknamed "the slave breaker." Douglass writes that eventually he was close to being broken in body, soul, and spirit. "My natural elasticity was crushed, my intellect languished, the disposition to read departed, the cheerful sparking that lingered about my eyes died; the dark night of slavery closed in upon me."[4] Fortunately, Douglass found the strength to fight back. But just barely.

Despair is one of the saddest words in the dictionary. It holds hands with defeat; it is the root of the word desperation. It is what brings some people to the place where, like Demby, they simply quit. As members of the human family, we must be on the lookout for those who are walking too close to this temptation. For some, the desperation is glaringly evident, but for many it easily escapes detection. I love the fact that Thoreau inserts the word "quiet" before the word desperation—we lead lives of *quiet* desperation. No loud shouting for most, not even for Demby. The heart has retreated into hopelessness.

3. Douglass, *Narrative of the Life of Frederick Douglass, an American Slave,* 32.

4. Ibid., 63.

We need to pay more attention to each other and offer whatever encouragement, large or small, we can. After all, to be truly human implies the importance of an investment in all humanity. We must remind each other that God has a purpose for our lives, and that even though we are tempted to believe that all is lost, we must hold on and fight to make the most of this precious, fragile gift God has given to us.

> Therefore, we do not lose heart. Though outwardly we are wasting away, yet inwardly we are being renewed day by day. For our light and momentary troubles are achieving for us an eternal glory that far outweighs them all. (2 Corinthians 4:16–17, NIV)

Filled with Straw

We are the hollow men
We are the stuffed men
Leaning together
Headpiece filled with straw. Alas!
Our dried voices, when
We whisper together
Are quiet and meaningless
As wind in dry grass. . .[1]

—T. S. Eliot, "The Hollow Men"

When I read T.S. Eliot's "The Hollow Men" to my students, I end with a pause. The words need time to set in, for me and my students. After a brief silence, I'll often say to them, "If I could write something half as good as that in my lifetime, I'll be perfectly content." I smile and scan the room to gauge their reactions.

Some students will smile or nod in agreement. Some will roll their eyes. Some will already have fearful looks, knowing that, soon, they'll be responsible for articulating some semblance of meaning from the poem. They quickly turn to the text looking for answers. But others—and these are the ones that are disconcerting—will have found this moment of silence (or the reading of the poem) uncomfortable, and rather than engaging, will turn to their cell phones as a distraction. Ugh.

I explain how Eliot is writing this poem to a post-war generation that is lost. His audience (and subject) was a generation of people living without meaning in a world that had completely changed. War had come and gone, but the impact lingered. Eliot's poem depicts this world as lost, aimless, "behaving as the wind behaves"; they

1. Eliot, "The Hollow Men," *The Complete Poems and Plays*, 56.

were empty, stark, and being carried along rather than contributing. They weren't in solitude—Eliot uses words which point to groups of people ("leaning together")—and yet, everything still feels isolated and alone. They were falling into line with the patterns of the world around them, and it's not a pretty picture.

Nearly a century later, the world has changed, but I think Eliot's words still resonate. Wars have come and gone and come again, but now we rarely take notice; we've become jaded. Terrible atrocities happen daily and are quickly forgotten with each fresh news cycle. Facebook, Twitter, Snapchat and Instagram serve as diversions in the meantime, and although they seem to keep us connected, as Eliot states, "We grope together / And avoid speech."[2] Today, we too often show our appreciation (or concern) for one another with smiley faces instead of smiling faces. And although we live in a world where we can know any and everything at the touch of a keypad, we only focus on what's "trending." Too often, we are hollow, following rather than leading, and behaving "as the wind behaves." And Eliot's warning stands:

> This is the way the world ends
> This is the way the world ends
> This is the way the world ends
> Not with a bang but a whimper.[3]

> Do not conform to the pattern of this world, but be transformed by the renewing of your mind. Then you will be able to test and approve what God's will is—his good, pleasing and perfect will. (Romans 12:2, NIV)

2. Eliot, "The Hollow Men," *The Complete Poems and Plays*, 58.
3. Ibid., 59.

Service or Selfishness?

When I consider how my light is spent
    Ere half my days in this dark world and wide,
    And that one talent which is death to hide
Lodged with me useless, 'though my soul more bent

To serve therewith my Maker, and present
    My true account, lest he returning chide;
    "Doth God exact day-labour, light denied?"
I fondly ask. But Patience, to prevent

That murmur, soon replies, "God doth not need
    Either man's work or his own gifts. Who best
    Bear his mild yoke, they serve him best. His state
Is Kingly: thousands at his bidding speed,
    And post o'er land and ocean without rest;
    They also serve who only stand and wait."[1]

—JOHN MILTON, "SONNET 19"

Acts of service are my wife's love language. On a day when she is working long hours, she may leave me a specific list of things she'd love for me to do around the house: clean the bathrooms, vacuum the carpets, wash the dishes, and do laundry. However, if it's a beautiful day outside, I may opt to mow the lawn and do some weeding in the garden. It's still housework, right? It's work around the house, and it needs to be done. Is this service?

1. Milton, "Sonnet 19," *The Oxford Book of English Verse, 1250-1900*, 342.

The National Honor Society is built on four pillars: Scholarship, Leadership, Character, and Service. At my high school, NHS students peer tutor for hours upon hours around our building each day. Some host shadow students as they come visit our school. Others come to extracurricular activities to set up, clean up, or support the staff in a variety of other ways. There is no shortage of help early in the year, but as more and more students complete their mandatory service hour requirements, the offers for help become less and less frequent. Meanwhile, these juniors and seniors proudly and happily write "NHS Member" on their college applications. Is this service?

Each year, our school sends out several service trips to locations both domestic and internationally. On a couple occasions, I've led twenty-five students on a trip to Jamaica to work alongside a deaf community for ten days in January. Each morning, they bicker over who will complete certain tasks. Painting is fun, but some students want a tan, so they argue for yard work. Others complain about having to pour concrete for a second straight day. Three hours into the work day, a chorus of complaints arises as students are tired, hungry, and want to know when they will be finished for the day. Community members from Jamaica, eager to make the American students happy, encourage them to take the afternoon off—the students readily oblige. Service?

Finally, in the poem above, John Milton is frustrated with the steady decline of his eyesight. He prays to God to restore his sight so that he can better serve God. Milton feels as though his talents are minimized by his disability, and he argues he is less able to do God's will without sight. His initial frustration with his situation, and his questioning of God's plan, seem to connect to the scenarios above—in each situation, there's a struggle between the call to service and our natural selfishness. However, in Milton's case, God sets him straight.

At the volta in the poem, Milton realizes the error in his thinking. God reminds him that God does not *need* Milton's service; honoring God with service isn't a favor to God or a bargaining chip. Rather, in response to his complaints, Milton receives a response that serves as a statement to all: "Who best / Bear his mild yoke, they serve him best." Simply put, service and selfishness are not compatible. True service is putting our own desires second and humbly doing what is needed to serve others, not dictating the terms or reaping personal rewards along the way. Service needn't be suffering, but it does call for humility, understanding of those served, and sacrifice. It's not about recognition, a tan, or any other self-motivated interest; however, it also needn't be misery. Once we learn to serve humbly and selflessly, fulfillment will follow. Nobel Prize winner Rabindranath Tagore says it beautifully: "I slept and dreamt that life was joy. I awoke and saw that life was service. I acted, and behold, service was joy."[2]

> The greatest among you will be your servant. For those who exalt themselves will be humbled, and those who humble themselves will be exalted. (Matthew 23:11–13, NIV)

---

2. Shea, *The Spiritual Wisdom of the Gospels for Christian Preachers and Teachers*, 193.

Suffering

Monster

> Was I then, a monster, a blot upon the earth, from which all men fled and whom all men disowned? I cannot describe to you the agony that these reflections inflicted upon me: I tried to dispel them, but sorrow only increased with knowledge.[1]
>
> —MARY SHELLEY, *FRANKENSTEIN*

One evening each week, I travel with three others to a prison near my city where we hold a book club. The first time I walked through the series of gates and glanced up at the barbed wire latticed above the prison walls, all my preconceptions about prison were confirmed. The men who gather with us are almost all "lifers"—many of them are in their thirties and forties, although almost all of them became prisoners at a much younger age. I cannot do justice to the profound effect these weekly visits have on my heart and soul, let alone to my views about restorative justice legislation. The men come each week so grateful for this respite from the routine and always eager to listen and share. Recently, we discussed *Frankenstein,* the classic book by Mary Shelley. Contrary to all the cartoons and inaccurate movies based on this book, *Frankenstein* is a powerful, thrilling story, and as the author puts it, a depiction of "a modern Prometheus." Frankenstein himself is the creator of the monster. He is a scientist who wants to play God and create his own "Adam." But when he sees the results of his experiment, he is horrified and runs away from the monster, hoping to never encounter him again. Later in the book, the monster finds Frankenstein and pleads with him to create a companion. The monster is miserable and lonely and intelligent and full of potential for good. However, in his desire

---

1. Shelley, *Frankenstein,* 128.

to make friends, he accidentally kills a child in an attempt to stifle the child's screams of fear at his appearance.

One of the men in our group began the second week of our discussion of this book by making a request. "Could we not call this creation of Frankenstein's a *monster* as we talk about him tonight? It hurts me to think of someone with so many gifts and so much potential in that way." Several objected, and one prisoner said indignantly, "He *did* kill a *child*! Here we call that a monster." The first man responded, "True. . . and what do people on the outside call *us*? What are *you*? What am *I*? Do we want to be identified only by our monstrosities? Isn't there at least some monster in any person on this earth?"

The room where we had gathered got very quiet.

His words touched me deeply. If we are all completely honest with ourselves, we must come to the conclusion that we, too, are capable of monstrosities, if not in action, then certainly in thought. Have you ever wished for someone else's failure? Have you ever hated someone so intensely that it scared you? Have you ever participated in something that was so ugly and so dirty that you felt a shame that still haunts you to this day?

We must be careful not to allow the burden of sin and guilt to destroy our belief in the power of God's forgiving grace. One of the most important lessons these men have taught me is that God is able to erase the stains that erode our relationship with him, with others, and especially with ourselves. No one is unredeemable. But before we can receive grace, we have to be willing to face our own inclination toward evil and cry out to our creator, who, unlike Frankenstein, is more than willing and able to deliver us.

> What a wretched man I am! Who will rescue me from this body of death? (Romans 7:24, NIV)

Meaningless

> Rosewater was twice as smart as Billy, but he and Billy were dealing with similar crises in similar ways. They had both found life meaningless, partly because of what they had seen in war. Rosewater, for instance, had shot a fourteen-year-old fireman, mistaking him for a German soldier. So it goes. And Billy had seen the greatest massacre in European history, which was the fire-bombing of Dresden. So it goes.
>
> So they were trying to re-invent themselves and their universe.[1]
>
> —KURT VONNEGUT, *SLAUGHTERHOUSE-FIVE*

Slaughterhouse-Five is the story of a man named Billy Pilgrim, who is "tall and weak, and shaped like a bottle of Coca-Cola."[2] He is far too sensitive and inept to be a good soldier, but he was drafted for military service in WWII. After he is taken prisoner by the Germans and witnesses the saturation bombing of Dresden by the Allies, he suffers a nervous collapse and is hospitalized.

In the quote above, we are given a glimpse of two hospital roommates—Rosewater, who has killed a fourteen-year-old boy by mistake, and Billy, who has been abused by his captors and even his fellow soldiers because of his inability to cope with the demands of being a soldier in the face of vast inhumanities on both sides. Billy is quickly marked as a weakling, an easy target.

As you get into the book, you find yourself with Billy in several different time periods that come and go like nightmare sequences. Sometimes he is in his pre-war world with a father

---

1. Vonnegut, *Slaughterhouse-Five*, 128.
2. Ibid., 30.

who threw him into a pool to teach him to swim by the "sink or swim" method. (Billy had to be rescued from the bottom of the pool because he preferred to sink.) And then, suddenly, he is in the post-war world, married and a successful ophthalmologist who finds himself wanting to sleep and fighting back tears which come unannounced. Then, oddly, he is whisked off to a planet his troubled mind has created called Tralfamadore, where he is put on display, naked, in a kind of zoo and considered a marvelous specimen from another world. Here he learns that one of the remarkable things about human beings is that they think they have free will, while all the Trafalmadorians know they are just "bugs in amber." And then back to war.

Vonnegut has a small "chorus" that he repeats in the book over and over again. It occurs every time he talks about anyone dying. Three small words, which sum up his philosophy of life: "So it goes." As I read this book, I can't help feeling that those three words are a kind of shrug—a fatalistic submission to the inevitable end of basically everything. It makes me think of another writer—the author of Ecclesiastes, probably Solomon, who similarly summarizes his philosophy of life with three words: "All is meaningless."

Ecclesiastes is a book that has long puzzled Christians, and some have even questioned its validity as holy scripture. Solomon, the great king of Israel, who had it all—riches, intelligence, even peace in his time—writes this book near the end of his life and basically dismisses everything. Listen to one of his pronouncements: "Yet when I surveyed all that my hands had done and what I had toiled to achieve, everything was meaningless, a chasing after the wind; nothing was gained under the sun."

How can this be? One can believe that a beleaguered man like Billy Pilgrim, clearly suffering from PTSD, finds life empty having lived through the ravages and insanity of war. But Solomon? He had it all! How can two men who are such polar opposites come to the same conclusion about life?

Perhaps to answer this question, we need to look at what they have in common. Both men despair because they have, as Solomon says, "lived beneath the sun," or as Vonnegut says, tried to "re-invent the universe." And in that futile process, both men have managed to leave God out of the picture even though Solomon began his reign with a glorious intimacy with God. The message comes through loud and clear: we cannot do this thing called life without God. He is our great, often unacknowledged, hunger and our only lasting path to meaning and peace.

> But in your hearts revere Christ as Lord. Always be prepared to give an answer to everyone who asks you to give a reason for the hope that you have. But do this with gentleness and respect. (1 Peter 3:15, NIV)

Part of God's Plan

> I wish those people who write so glibly about this being
> a holy War, and the orators who talk so much about go-
> ing on no matter how long the War lasts and what it may
> mean, could see a case—to say nothing of ten cases—of
> mustard gas in its early stages—could see the poor things
> burned and blistered all over with great mustard-colored
> suppurating blisters, with blind eyes—sometimes tempo-
> rarily, sometimes permanently—all sticky and stuck to-
> gether, and always fighting for breath, with voices a mere
> whisper, saying that their throats are closing and they
> know they will choke. . . and yet people persist in saying
> God made the War. . . .[1]

—VERA BRITTAIN, *TESTAMENT OF YOUTH*

Romans 8:28 is a very popular verse. It comes in handy for Christians at times when they don't know what to say. Often, it's used
as a band-aid for all suffering. When a bad diagnosis is given,
when a friend passes away, or when financial disaster strikes,
people offer the verse up as a cure for all of life's ills: "And we
know that in all things God works for the good of those who love
him, who have been called according to his purpose." Essentially,
we encourage people, when they are hurting most, to cheer up
because it's all a part of God's plan! Yet too often in those moments, this verse isn't helpful.

It's not wrong. All things do happen in accordance with God's
will. We don't always understand why things happen, and we need
to have faith that there *is* a greater purpose. But it's not generally the
message people need to hear in the midst of their trials. Not only is
it not helpful, but it can do more harm than good.

1. Brittain, *Testament of Youth*, 395.

Vera Brittain makes this point in her memoir, *Testament of Youth*. While World War I was destroying her country and robbing her of her loved ones, the last thing she wanted to hear was how "God made the War." She describes, in brutal detail, victims of gas attacks, and she questions how anyone can come to the conclusion that the War is holy. She sees far more of Satan's handiwork than God's.

Many of the survivors of World War I came to the same conclusion. Romans 8:28 couldn't explain away the atrocities they survived. The post-war generation struggled with how a perfect God could possibly have allowed such a terrible event. It's hard to blame them. And a century later, when brothers and sisters in Christ face challenges large and small, this message can be equally discomforting.

When disaster strikes, perhaps Christians shouldn't immediately come to the situation trying to explain or justify. The time for reflection and understanding may eventually come, but rather than immediately flipping to Romans 8, perhaps looking a few chapters further might be more appropriate. "Rejoice with those who rejoice; mourn with those who mourn," Paul writes. Don't rush to explain away pain and suffering. To borrow the words of my former pastor, sometimes we need to offer *solidarity*, not *solutions*.

Listen to the pain of those who feel pain. Acknowledge how hard things can be. Let God's love do his work through you.

> Rejoice with those who rejoice; mourn with those who mourn. (Romans 12:15, NIV)

Standard Equipment

> I knew that she was going to die and I prayed that she
> would not. Don't let her die. Oh, God, please don't let her
> die. I'll do anything for you if you won't let her die. Please,
> please, please, dear God, don't let her die. Dear God, don't
> let her die. Please please please make her not die. . . I'll do
> anything you say if you don't let her die. . . . [1]

—ERNEST HEMINGWAY, *A FAREWELL TO ARMS*

When my Modern Fiction class begins our study of *A Farewell to
Arms*, we spend some time watching a video on the life of Hemingway. The students are intrigued by his macho "grace under pressure"
philosophy, and his hardcore resistance to belief in God. Believing
in God is a sign of weakness. When someone once asked him about
his views on prayer, Hemingway quipped, "Our Nada who art in
heaven, nada be thy name."[2] So when, near the end of the book,
the main character, Frederic, who is loosely based on Hemingway
himself and his experiences in WWI, begins to desperately pray,
my students object. They think it is a step away from the way the
character has been portrayed throughout the book—rejecting the
priest's belief in God, ardently agreeing with his beloved Catherine
that their relationship was as close to religion as they would ever
get, and so on. Furthermore, my students assert that it is a betrayal
of Hemingway's own beliefs to bring prayer into the picture at all.
What happens to grace under pressure, the stiff upper lip and all that
when Frederick falls apart in this pathetic manner?

So I tell them about something that happened to me several
years ago. Our five-year-old son had just had extensive, risky sur-
gery, and he was asleep in the ICU. I was spending the night there

1. Hemingway, *A Farewell to Arms*, 330.
2. Crisman, *Biography—Ernest Hemingway: Wrestling with Life.*

at his bedside with a curtain drawn between us and another patient, a young girl, just a few feet away. During the night, I got up to get a cup of coffee and met her mother, who was also keeping a vigil beside her daughter that night. We shared our children's ailments with each other and both shook our heads in disbelief at why children suffer.

"How do you cope?" she asked me at one point in our conversation.

"I pray a lot."

She snorted. "A lot of good that does. Pray? If there was a God—and I don't believe there is—his allowing children to suffer and die makes him nothing more than a heartless monster."

And she left, clearly annoyed by the whole conversation. But during the night, her daughter died—her disease made her lungs fill up with water, and basically she drowned. And as the little girl gasped for air, her mother was praying a prayer very similar to Hemingway's. "Please, God, save her! Oh *please*, God. . ."

This is one reason, I tell my students, that Hemingway is a brilliant and insightful writer. Had Frederic suddenly converted? No. He was a desperate man who was grasping at any possible way out of the darkness. He couldn't help himself.

And neither can we. It is part of our "soul's standard equipment"[3] to borrow a phrase from Dr. Cornelius Plantinga, to call out to the one who created us in the first place. "Whom have I in heaven but you?" cries out the psalmist in Psalm 73. When the world is falling apart, we look for someone to rescue us. And God's promise is that he *will*. That doesn't necessarily mean we will get our child back. But we get *him*—and that is our real salvation. It is one of the hardest and most important truths we must learn this side of heaven.

> From the ends of the earth I call to you, I call as my heart
> grows faint; lead me to the rock that is higher than I.
> (Psalm 61:2, NIV)

3. Plantinga, *Engaging God's World*, 6.

Love

Religion or Relationship?

We know nothing of religion here: we think only of Christ.
We know nothing of speculation. Come and see.[1]

—C. S. Lewis, *The Great Divorce*

The Great Divorce is a book about second chances. People who have died have gone either to heaven or to hell, but those who have gone to hell get an opportunity to travel to the edge of heaven where they are invited by someone already in heaven to reconsider what kept them from getting there. In chapter five, we see a man who has gone to hell because he turned away from all the most important truths about Christianity—truths like that Jesus was the Son of God, that he came to save us, that he died to set us free from the finality of death. Ironically, the man in hell was a theologian. Instead of embracing these essential teachings, he put his efforts into creating a much more "palatable" religion, one that people would find easier to swallow, and before he died he became immensely popular for his radical speculations and easy discarding of the foundations of faith.

He is met by a friend who hung onto his beliefs and went to heaven. The friend is trying to convince the theologian to return to his love for *Christ himself*. It is not, he tells him, about *religion*. It is about *relationship*. For some reason, this chapter brings to mind for me the line from John Lennon's song "Imagine" where he suggests all the things that would make the world more wonderful, including no religion.

In my classroom, I have a small poster that says simply: "Christianity is a *relationship*." One might say it is not so much a "what" as a "who." To my way of thinking, that is the most notable and compelling reason for choosing to become a Christian. In all religions, there is a grasping for truth, a reaching up for some way to

1. Lewis, *The Great Divorce,* 42.

find meaning in this world, for something big enough to stake our lives upon. What is unique about Christianity is that it is the only religion where someone reaches back to us. This came about through the incarnation—God becoming one of us, Jesus "moving into the neighborhood" so to speak. No other religion, no other deity does this. It is an act of outrageous love. It is intensely personal.

The encounter that is recorded in this chapter is one of many throughout the book. Each one concludes either with a choice to return to hell, a choice to surrender a particular idol and proceed to heaven, or simply a continuation of the conversation, leaving the reader to wonder what its resolution will likely be. I find it interesting that this is the only encounter where the one sent from heaven despairs of the effort and turns away. One is reminded of C.S. Lewis's claim that God does not send anyone to hell—the door to hell is "locked from the inside."[2]

> For God so loved the world that he gave his one and only Son, that whoever believes in him shall not perish, but have eternal life. (John 3:16, NIV)

2. Lewis, *The Problem of Pain*, 124.

More Than Conquerors

I am the master of my fate,

I am the captain of my soul . . . [1]

—WILLIAM ERNEST HENLEY, "INVICTUS"

These are the final lines from a famous poem, quoted often. Interestingly, it is considered the only "successful" poem William Ernest Henley ever wrote. The word "invictus" is Latin for unconquered, and the poem itself represents the kind of Victorian stoicism that was a part of the world Henley lived in. It has been used at many graduations, as a kind of admonishing "send off" to young graduates entering their futures, a kind of "go off and make your destiny and take charge" kind of message. In 1941, Winston Churchill quoted this to the House of Commons as they faced the horrors of WWII together. Timothy McVeigh, the Oklahoma City bomber of 1995, quoted these last lines from the poem just before he was executed on June 1, 2001. President Barack Obama read the poem at his friend Nelson Mandela's funeral in 2013. There is even a movie titled *Invictus* based on the poem. In the movie, Mandela gives a copy of the poem to the captain of the South African rugby team for inspiration, but in real life he gave an excerpt from a speech by Teddy Roosevelt.

It is clearly a popular sentiment. However, I would suggest that despite its popularity, it is a lie. Likely an unpopular declaration, but everything in the Bible contradicts it. In fact, those who believed they were the masters of their own fate and the captains of their own souls were some of the saddest characters in the biblical story. Take Saul, for example. From all appearances, Saul was *the* man for the job of Israel's first king. Everyone thought so—especially Saul. But his stubborn insistence on doing things *his* way instead of *God's* way

---

1. Henley, "Invictus," *Lyra Heroica: A Book of Verse for Boys*, 97.

resulted in disaster for him and his family. Or take Nebuchadnezzar, the haughty, arrogant king of Babylon. He was humbled by God by being forced to live with the wild animals and eat grass, but eventually he was restored to his throne because he sincerely proclaimed: "God's dominion is an eternal dominion. . . . I will now glorify the King of heaven because everything he does is right. . . . And those who walk in pride he is able to humble." (Daniel 4:34–37)

Does this mean we should not dream dreams for the future or acknowledge our own ability to choose? Not at all. But we must remember that, in David Brooks' words, "To believe that you can be captain of your own life is to suffer the sin of pride. . . . Pride is building your happiness around your own accomplishments, using your work as the measure of your worth. It is believing that you can arrive at fulfillment on your own, driven by your own individual efforts."[2]

We must surrender the belief that we are capable of steering our own lives. The familiar first question and answer of the Heidelberg Catechism is: "What is your only comfort in life and in death?"[3] Hopefully you know the answer. It is all about dwelling in the awareness that you belong to someone bigger than yourself. And he, in his infinite love for us, will give our lives meaning and direction beyond what we could ever imagine.

> No, in all these things we are more than conquerors through him who loves us. (Romans 8:37, NIV)

2. Brooks, *The Road to Character*, 199.
3. Bierma, *The Theology of the Heidelberg Catechism*, 13.

How She's Treated

The difference between a lady and a flower girl is not how she behaves, but how she's treated.[1]

—George Bernard Shaw, *Pygmalion*

The Bible—the Old Testament in particular—is full of a lot of rules. The Israelites are given a blueprint of things that must be done in order to serve God. Often called commandments, they were issued to God's people directly from above, or through his prophets. Many seem obvious (and, for most, easy to follow):

"You shall not murder." (Ex. 20:13)

"Do not have sexual relations with your sister." (Lev. 18:9)

Some are a bit more difficult:

"You shall not covet your neighbor's house." (Ex. 20:17)

"Do not take advantage of each other." (Lev. 25:17)

Some feel outdated:

"If a slave has taken refuge with you, do not hand them over to their master." (Deut. 23:16)

"You shall not covet your neighbor's ox or donkey." (Ex. 20:17)

Some are just plain strange or oddly specific:

"Do not cut yourselves or shave the front of your heads for the dead." (Deut. 14:1)

"If a man marries a woman who becomes displeasing to him because he finds something indecent about her,

1. Shaw, *Pygmalion*, 80.

and he writes her a certificate of divorce, gives it to her and sends her from his house, and if after she leaves his house she becomes the wife of another man, and her second husband dislikes her and writes her a certificate of divorce, gives it to her and sends her from his house, or if he dies, then her first husband, who divorced her, is not allowed to marry her again." (Deut. 24:4)

All have (or had) a reason for their importance. Biblical scholars and pastors justify, explain, or contextualize all of these rules, and sermons are preached explaining how (or whether) the rules still apply today.

But there is one commandment that requires little explanation and no contextualizing to be understood. It's given first in the book of Leviticus, and again by Christ himself in the gospels: "Love your neighbor as yourself." A simple enough commandment to understand, it's often the subject of children's sermons or dropped casually as the moral of a Sunday school lesson. It sounds simple. But it's a law each and every one of us need to be reminded of every single day.

In his play *Pygmalion*, George Bernard Shaw shows us why. Like many in our world, protagonist Eliza Doolittle lives in poverty; we meet her selling flowers for pennies a bunch. Everywhere she goes, she is looked down upon. She can't get a better job because her appearance and language immediately give away her class. As a result, no one wants anything to do with her. These are barriers she can't control; no matter how hard she works or how determined she is—no matter how much she tries to follow the rules society says will lead to success—she will always be a flower girl and will always be treated like a flower girl. The way others view her is a picture of the brokenness in our world.

A neighborly action brings about her transformation within the story. She learns, through the kindness of another character, that the "difference between a lady and a flower girl is not how she behaves, but how she is treated." One major character, looking past her position, treats her with love and respect, and it changes everything. We are called to go and do likewise.

Truly I tell you, whatever you did for one of the least of these brothers and sisters of mine, you did for me. (Matthew 25:40, NIV)

Not Enough

"What's this call, this sperit? It's love. . . . An' I says to myself, 'Don't you love Jesus?' Well, I thought an' thought an' finally I says, 'No, I don't know nobody named Jesus, I know a bunch of stories, but I only love people. . . . I figgered about the Holy Sperit and the Jesus road. I figgered, 'maybe it's all men an' all women we love; maybe that's the Holy Sperit—the human sperit. . . .'"[1]

—JOHN STEINBECK, *THE GRAPES OF WRATH*

Jim Casy is a radical character in Steinbeck's book. He is a former preacher who went off into the wilderness and returned a new kind of preacher—Steinbeck's kind. The message he preaches is humanism, and the hope that he holds out to the world is all about our responsibility to one another.

There is a part of me that really appreciates this. And I love the message of this book, which is all about becoming stronger by taking care of one another and not just pursuing self-interest. But the thing is, we just aren't that good. When we think about loving other people, we are full of noble intentions. We treat our friends well, and we even give up our precious time for service projects sometimes. But when it comes to the people who just get under our skin and make us want to scratch away the irritation, we have a harder time of it. Try as we may, there comes a point where we either avoid them or lash out against them in frustration or anger.

It takes something bigger than the human spirit.

Jesus had to step in so that we could get a glimpse of what real love looks like. I am reminded of one of the final scenes of a favorite movie of mine, *Dead Man Walking*. The nun who has been assigned to mentor a young man named Matthew Poncelet

1. Steinbeck, *The Grapes of Wrath*, 32.

is trying to prepare him for his execution—but even more, to prepare him to meet God. In the end, he finally confesses to the crime he has denied all along and sobs, "God knows the truth about me." As he is waiting to be taken to his death, he asks the nun if she will be one of the witnesses. She nods, and says, "Christ is here. I'll be the face of love for you, Matthew Poncelet. The truth will set you free."[2] How can she love this man who raped a young woman and killed her boyfriend and refused to take responsibility for creating hell for their families? God gave her the ability to see him through the eyes of Christ, who is the author of love. And it was the work of the Holy Spirit that brought forth Matthew's "Holy Spirit tears"—the clear indication that his regret at being cornered for his sins had moved into repentance, which consequently allowed him to be found as a child of God.

People are usually a bit uncomfortable with the line from the hymn "Amazing Grace" that says, "Amazing grace / how sweet the sound / that saved a wretch like me."[3] A *wretch*? Isn't that pushing it a little? But the truth is, we human beings are both beautiful and despicable to varying degrees. It takes something bigger than people to erase the ugliness. It takes Someone bigger.

Jesus said, "I am the way, the truth, and the life." (John 14:6a, NIV)

2. Robbins, *Dead Man Walking*.
3. Wesley, "Amazing Grace," 691.

I Should Much Rather Have . . .

A mind like this I need for a son? A *heart* I need for a son,
a *soul* I need for a son, *compassion* I want from my son,
righteousness, mercy, strength to suffer and carry pain,
that I want from my son, not a mind without a soul![1]

—CHAIM POTOK, *THE CHOSEN*

Many parents are vigilant about checking on their children's
grades—particularly in high school, when grades play such a big
role in determining scholarships and acceptance to prestigious
universities and colleges. In the process, though, how a child is
faring socially or emotionally or spiritually can often take second
place—or get lost all together.

In Chaim Potok's first novel, *The Chosen*, Rabbi Saunders leads
the Hasidic community in Brooklyn, New York, with integrity and
compassion. He is highly respected as a *tzaddik*—a bridge between
God and the people he serves. By tradition, the eldest son of the
rabbi's family is destined (chosen) to inherit the father's position
after his death. Danny is that son. What makes Danny unique—
and particularly appealing to the people in his community—is that
he is a genius. He possesses a photographic memory and a brilliant
mind, and he is able to memorize and recite from the Talmud and
Torah with astonishing accuracy, even correcting his father's inten-
tional errors in his sermons.

But Rabbi Saunders is not satisfied with this. He tells Danny's
friend that at an early age his son was able to read and remember
all that he had read. He came to his father with pride and delight
in his discovered gift, and his father trembled. Why? Because
Danny had just read and recited a story of great tragedy and pain,
but he was not moved by it.

1. Potok, *The Chosen*, 264.

Most of us have seen the fantastic movie *The Wizard of Oz*, or perhaps some stage reproduction of its basic story. However, few have read the actual book by L. Frank Baum. In the book version, the Tin Man tells the story of how he became tin: he was a real man once, but a wicked witch did not want him to love the woman he had chosen, so she cursed his axe, causing it to slip and destroy parts of his body over and over again. This ultimately forced him to recreate himself into a man made out of tin. The scarecrow says to him, "I think you are wrong to want a heart. It makes most people unhappy. If you only knew it—you are in luck *not* to have a heart." And even the Wizard tells him later, "Hearts will never be practical until they can be made unbreakable." But the Tin Man declares adamantly, "Once I had brains, and a heart also; so having had them both, I should much rather have a heart."[2]

But it need not be one or the other. Brains may get us a scholarship, a career, status, and financial success down the line, and the heart can give us the passion and love that gives us direction to use what we have acquired for the good of the world. Ultimately love is always the best motivator, the channel our brains should travel in order to seek direction and purpose for what we learn. It is this channel that irrigates our lives with the compassion, righteousness, mercy, and strength to suffer that turns our gaze inevitably to the cross. Robert Pierce, founder of *World Vision* and *Samaritan's Purse*, wrote a note in his Bible after one of his mission trips. It has since become famous: "Let my heart be broken with the things that break the heart of God."[3] It is perhaps one of the most Christ-like prayers we can ever pray.

> Above all else, guard your heart, for everything you do
> flows from it. (Proverbs 4:23, NIV)

2. Baum, *The Wizard of Oz*, 33.

3. Spangler, *Praying the Attributes of God*, 203.

What Love Looks Like

> What you tell me about in the nights. That is not love. That is only passion and lust. When you love you wish to do things for. You wish to sacrifice for. You wish to serve.[1]
>
> —ERNEST HEMINGWAY, *A FAREWELL TO ARMS*

This quote, spoken to a young soldier by a priest, is one of the best definitions of love I have ever come upon. It's ironic that it comes from Hemingway, who was married four times and once commented when a woman he had just ended an affair with jumped from the second story of a building: "She was the first woman who ever literally fell for me."[2] In today's world, this man who was, according to all who knew him, "never without a woman in his life" would certainly have been targeted by the #MeToo movement. Near the end of his life, Hemingway wrote a memoir of his early years of writing called *A Moveable Feast.* In it, he confesses that the only woman he probably ever really loved was his first wife, Hadley. This was the woman who was the most forgiving, who supported his career with dedication and encouragement, who put her own interests on hold for his sake, and who, after he wanted a divorce so that he could marry another woman, wrote him that she wished him well and forgave him.

Physical attraction, mutual interests, and sparkling personality are certainly compelling reasons to begin a romance. In the early years of dating or courtship, there is understandably a high level of intensity and pursuit. Gifts and notes and other small or large gestures of affection are part of the dance that occurs between two people who are considering committing to each other. And yet, divorce rates continue to soar, and the reluctance to marry is far more prevalent now than it was for our parents' or grandparents' generations.

1. Hemingway, *A Farewell to Arms,* 72.
2. Crisman, *Biography–Ernest Hemingway: Wrestling with Life.*

Perhaps it is because in a self-actualization culture where we are told to pursue the greatness that surely lies within each and every one of us, our agenda reverses the direction of the priest's quote to justify doing things for ourselves, sacrificing and serving for the sake of our own best interests and fulfillment. There's a reason, after all, that Jesus admonished us to "love our neighbors as ourselves"—most of us are pretty darn good at loving ourselves.

I have a friend who is battling a debilitating illness. Her body is betraying her in countless ways, and she has just taken to using a walker to get around, even though, in her words, "I don't feel old enough to need a walker." Her husband has been at her side throughout, taking her to appointments, putting in a chair lift on their stair railing so that she can still sleep in her own bedroom, running all the errands she used to handle. Now he is struggling as well, having just been diagnosed with cancer. Every day is a struggle, and they are together trying to make life as "normal" as possible. She told me recently that she was lying awake in bed one night, thinking about their wedding day—how innocent they were, and how much fun they had, and how they had managed to get through some terrible tragedies as their lives together unfolded over the years. Her husband, lying beside her, was also awake, although she didn't know it until he said, "I've just been lying here thinking about our wedding day." This is what love looks like.

It is interesting, I think, that the character who gives the definition of love in Hemingway's novel is a priest. Frederic Henry, the young soldier the priest is speaking to, objects, claiming the celibate priest cannot really know what love is. The priest suggests that perhaps they are not really so different. And although Frederic never pursues this (nor does Hemingway), I believe that he inadvertently makes an important point. Love seeks to pour itself out. At the beginning it may look more lavish and flashy, but in the end it presents itself as a steady affirmation of promises made and kept, a hopeful pursuit of ways to "do things for," sacrifice, and serve. God's love for us revealed through Jesus is the ultimate example—we do well to imitate him as best we can.

We love because he first loved us. (1 John 4:19, NIV)

Faithfulness

Best-laid Schemes

But Mousie, thou art no thy lane,
In proving foresight may be vain:
The best-laid schemes o' mice an' men
Gang aft agley,
An' lea'e us nought but grief an' pain,
For promis'd joy![1]

—ROBERT BURNS, "TO A MOUSE"

"Elsie, after your grandma?"

"Oooh, I like that! Put it on the list. How about Cameron for a boy?"

"Nope. Sorry. Veto. Reminds me of a student I don't want to be reminded of."

"Oliver?"

"Hmmm... Oliver... Ollie... alright, I don't mind that. Put it on the list."

On road trips, my wife and I would talk about the names of our future children. We had a plan. We'd get married and have three kids—two girls and a boy ideally (but obviously, we knew that was out of our control). A decade ago, my wife and I had it all figured out. Little did we know. . . .

After years of trying and failing, buying and being disappointed by negative pregnancy tests, arguments, doctor appointments, and tears, our plans were shot. But that didn't stop us from making plans: Adoption? If so, international or domestic? Foster care? In vitro fertilization? We explored every possibility.

1. Burns, "To A Mouse," *Poems, Chiefly in the Scottish Dialect,* 140.

149

We finally decided we'd visit the fertility center—again, to explore *our* options. We settled on a series of treatments. It would cost tens of thousands of dollars (which we had, of course, begun to plan for) and require a lot of invasive treatments, but we had to *do* something. We continued to make plans. But God had other plans.

The evening before our IVF appointment—the appointment where all of our planning would begin to take shape—my wife took one last pregnancy test. For the first time in years, we expected nothing. We hadn't planned for a positive test. Rather, our plans had shifted to the next morning's appointment, and we were prepared to move forward. But, the test did read positive. All of our planning was again tossed aside. We cancelled the appointment. Excitedly, we realized that our plans meant nothing.

And I'm continually reminded of this daily by our newborn daughter. If I plan to get to work early, she'll have a blowout diaper. If we try to plan for a good night's sleep, she'll have other ideas. When we plan for exhaustion and a restful tomorrow, she decides to sleep through the night. Our best laid plans are often tossed aside. And we've come to embrace it.

It doesn't stop us from planning. Like Robert Burns's mouse in the poem above, we will continue to prepare for a future that is completely out of our control. My wife and I have already started a college fund for our daughter. We'll continue to book doctor's appointments for our and her well-being. We even, occasionally, talk about the idea of having another child so she'll have a sibling. But we recognize that none of this is really in our control. And that's okay.

> "For I know the plans I have for you," declares the Lord,
> "plans to prosper you and not to harm you, plans to give
> you hope and a future." (Jeremiah 29:11, NIV)

Mystery

"...If you read one of these books a day, it would still take you almost ten years to finish."

"What's your point?"

"The world, even the smallest parts of it, is filled with things you don't know."

Wow. That was a huge idea. . . .

"Okay, so it's like each of these books is a mystery. Every book is a mystery. And if you read all the books ever written, it's like you've read one giant mystery. And no matter how much you learn, you just keep on learning there is so much more you need to learn."[1]

—SHERMAN ALEXIE, *THE ABSOLUTELY TRUE DIARY
OF A PART-TIME INDIAN*

When I first started teaching, nearly fifteen years ago, I was petrified of being in front of students without knowing all the answers. So, to avoid any possible discomfort, I prepared meticulously: I read author biographies, I read and reread texts before lessons, and I researched every possible discussion question I could find. Despite all of this, I still found myself regularly panicking as students would put me in a position of unknowing. I felt that, as the instructor in the class, I was responsible for having every answer to any question that might come my way.

I don't feel that way today. In fact, last year, while teaching a poem I've taught for over a decade, I had a student ask a question about a break in meter that blindsided me. I had taught the poem many times. I taught that particular student about meter and had

---

1. Alexie, *The Absolutely True Diary of a Part-Time Indian,* 97.

challenged all my students to ask questions about irregularity of meter or syntax and how it might have meaning—how had I never seen this before?

For a brief moment, I wanted to try to cover up my ignorance. There was a second or three when my former teaching self came through and was embarrassed for not being ready with an immediate answer. But I quickly realized how amazing it was that a poem I had read to classes at least fifty different times was still opening my eyes to new possibilities. It's become one of the challenges I issue my students—to try to find things *I've* never noticed before. Now, I get excited when I don't know all the answers.

Arnold Spirit comes to a similar conclusion in Alexie's *The Absolutely True Diary of a Part-Time Indian*. Just the idea of how much learning is possible gets him excited. (And if you've read the novel, you'll appreciate my euphemistic choice of words.) Rather than get frustrated, Arnold is amazed when his friend Gordy explains how reading a book doesn't bring answers; it exposes mystery: "No matter how much you learn, you just keep on learning there is so much more you need to learn."

It's the same with faith. Initially, recognizing that you don't have all the answers about God and how the world works is frightening or troubling. But eventually, acknowledging that you don't have all the answers about God and how the world works is liberating.

I still prepare thoroughly, and I still try to reread texts before standing in front of each class. But now, I'm not as worried. I actually enjoy times when my students ask me questions that I don't immediately have an answer for. I like it even more when they ask questions I have never considered asking. And similarly, I find God more and more amazing the more I acknowledge I don't have all the answers to bigger life questions. Wow. That is a huge idea.

> When I came to you, I did not come with eloquence or human wisdom as I proclaimed to you the testimony about God. For I resolved to know nothing while I was with you except Jesus Christ and him crucified. I came to you in weakness with great fear and trembling. My

message and my preaching were not with wise and per-
suasive words, but with a demonstration of the Spirit's
power, so that your faith might not rest on human wisdom, but on God's power. (1 Corinthians 2:1–5, NIV)

Faith

"If it's this River of Life you want to lay your pain in, then come up," the preacher said, "and lay your sorrow here. But don't be thinking this is the last of it because this old red river don't end here. This old red suffering stream goes on, you people, slow to the Kingdom of Christ."

While he was talking, a fluttering figure had begun to move forward with a kind of butterfly movement—an old woman with flapping arms whose head wobbled as if it might fall off any second. She managed to lower herself at the edge of the bank and let her arms churn in the water. Then she bent farther and pushed her face down in it and raised herself up finally, streaming wet; and still flapping, she turned a time or two in a blind circle until someone reached out and pulled her back into the group.

"She's been that way for thirteen years," a rough voice shouted.[1]

—FLANNERY O'CONNOR, "THE RIVER"

Flannery O'Connor is masterful at giving us glimpses into the human heart. But she uses a back door entrance. In this story, a traveling preacher is standing in the river, offering the kingdom to anyone who is willing to listen. There is a crowd there full of all kinds of people. Some are there for the show, hoping to see a healing. Some are complete cynics, like Mr. Paradise, who comes only to point out that the miracle of healing never comes.

There are some who seem to accept the preacher's invitation. One man dips his hand into the water; a woman lets her baby

---

1. O'Connor, *The Complete Stories*, 166.

splash its feet in the water. Another man even takes off his shoes and wades out a little way into the water and then wades back and puts his shoes back on. Who are these people? They are probably people like you and me, those who would *like* to believe in the possibility of what God could do with us, who would *like* to have more faith, who would *like* to go into the River of Life, but we only dabble in it. There is only the possibility of faith in us.

However, the clearly disabled, "fluttering figure" comes down to the river and completely submerges herself in its waters. And when she comes up, she is not healed; someone has to help her out. One of the cynics shouts, "She's been that way for thirteen years!" So she's a regular. But she never gets healed.

What is Flannery O'Connor doing here? I think that this moment is at the heart of the gospel, even though it is a back door revelation. Let me explain. My father suffered a stroke in his early seventies. The stroke crippled his left leg to the extent that he had to use a cane, and he had to have a special brace attached to his shoe to help him walk. He *hated* it—having always been an active sportsman, he now found himself losing a big chunk of his life. After his death, my mom told me that every night before bed, the two of them knelt at their bedside to pray. And his prayers always ended with a fervent request for healing: "Tomorrow, Lord, help me to rise out of this bed and leave my cane and brace behind." And every morning, he got up and discovered he had not been healed. "Son of a bitch!" he muttered. And then he put his brace on.

Why did he keep praying when his prayers weren't answered? Because he had faith that God *could* heal him if he chose to. Faith doesn't dabble. Faith puts it all on the line. Again and again.

> Now faith is being sure of what we hope for and certain
> of what we do not see. (Hebrews 11:1, NIV)

So It Goes

> All moments, past, present, and future, always have ex-
> isted, always will exist. The Tralfamadorians can look at
> all the different moments just the way we can look at a
> stretch of the Rocky Mountains, for instance. They can see
> how permanent all the moments are, and they can look at
> any moment that interests them. It is just an illusion we
> have here on Earth that one moment follows another one,
> like beads on a string, and that once a moment is gone it
> is gone forever.[1]
>
> —Kurt Vonnegut, *Slaughterhouse-Five*

Since my early Sunday school days, I've always been taught about
God through the three "omnis": omnipotent, omnipresent, and
omniscient. (I also distinctly remember feeling quite witty in middle school, arguing that Jesus was also omnivorous, having eaten
bread and fish.) When young, just being able to pronounce and define these three words was a big enough accomplishment; actually
comprehending them wasn't even on my radar.

God as omnipresent, or the idea that God is everywhere at
all times, is probably the easiest to reconcile. Although trinitarian
theology takes a bit to understand, once you accept the divinity of
the Holy Spirit, omnipresence comes readily.

God as omnipotent is trickier. If God is all-powerful, why
does he allow terrible things to happen in the world? Why doesn't
he just destroy Satan with the snap of a finger? These questions
can become troubling, especially when facing personal or family
challenges, or when watching a news filled with poverty, war, and
government corruption.

1. Vonnegut, *Slaughterhouse-Five*, 34.

One of the ways to come to terms with these troubling omnipotence-created questions is to take solace in God's omniscience. We may not have the answers, but our all-knowing God does. God sees all of history: past, present, and future. He knows how the story ends, and that's reassuring. And this concept is not too dissimilar to the way Kurt Vonnegut describes the Tralfamadorians, the alien species that kidnaps protagonist Billy Pilgrim in *Slaughterhouse-Five*. He explains how the "Tralfamadorians can look at all the different moments [in time] just the way we can look at a stretch of the Rocky Mountains," never focusing on the present alone.

Vonnegut's use of this concept in his novel is intriguing. Vonnegut reveals how Billy Pilgrim and the Tralfamadorians deal with death or suffering. Billy explains, "when a Tralfamadorian sees a corpse, all he thinks is that the dead person is in bad condition in that particular moment, but that the same person is just fine in plenty of other moments. Now, when I myself hear that somebody is dead, I simply shrug and say what the Tralfamadorians say about dead people, which is 'So it goes.'"[2]

At a glance, Billy's response seems a bit cold and uncaring, but with some thought, it's possible to view it as truly wonderful. Billy doesn't dwell on the sadness of death because there is so much happiness in a life to celebrate. Seeing all of time in an instant allows for a full picture of a life, rather than zeroing in on the moment of loss. Perhaps we could learn a bit from Billy's way of responding to the end of a life.

Of course, we don't see life as Billy Pilgrim does. We live in the present and react accordingly. And although we might find it reassuring to know that God does see all of history, it doesn't eliminate our present pain and suffering. However, there is another important distinction between the way we and the Tralfamadorians see life that can bring us joy: as Christians, we know that death is not the end. Our all-knowing, all-powerful, and ever-present God has prepared a second kingdom for us to look forward to, and if we accept his calling, we will be reunited with

2. Vonnegut, *Slaughterhouse-Five*, 34.

those whose lives we've mourned. Whereas the Tralfamadorians see time as a timeline, with a fixed beginning and end, we know that God, in his omnipotent and omniscient power, has extended the timeline indefinitely for anyone who accepts the gift that was earned through the death of Jesus. So it goes.

> Remember the former things, those of long ago;
>> I am God, and there is no other;
>> I am God, and there is none like me.
> I make known the end from the beginning,
>> from ancient times, what is still to come.
> I say, "My purpose will stand,
>> and I will do all that I please." (Isaiah 46:9–10, NIV)

Principles and Belief

> "Principles? Principles won't do. . . . No; you want a
> deliberate belief."[1]

—JOSEPH CONRAD, *HEART OF DARKNESS*

One of my best friends is a staunch atheist. He grew up in the
church but has since decided that belief in God doesn't make sense
for him. He's opted out. One day, in a conversation that moved
from hockey to beer to television to, eventually, religion (as our
discussions so often do), we hit a point in the discussion where
somehow—and I'm not sure what exactly brought it on—I tried to
validate my faith by asserting that it gives me a moral code. I was
trying to articulate how one of the reasons I value my belief in God
is it encourages me to do good in the world. He immediately shot
back: "Christians don't have a corner on morality."

And he was correct. Self-proclaimed agnostic Warren Buf-
fett has given billions to philanthropic causes, doing all kinds of
amazing and altruistic things with his wealth. Fellow billionaire
Bill Gates, founder of a foundation that does immense good in the
world, once said about church: "There's a lot more I could be doing
on a Sunday morning."[2] There are countless others who give their
time, energy, talent and other resources to serving humanity while
never professing it as an act of service to God. My friend was correct—Christians don't have a corner on morality.

But Christians do have a distinct calling toward morality,
one that is inherent in and integral to their *belief* in God. We do
good as an act of service to God, and it's because we believe we are
part of his redemptive plan. Unbelievers still do great things for
humanity and our environment (and that's still the work of God
as we're told in Philippians 2:13: "For it is God who is producing

1. Conrad, *Heart of Darkness*, 32.
2. Isaacson, "In Search of the Real Bill Gates."

in you both the desire and ability to do what pleases him"), but they do it more as a matter of principle, not within a larger system of belief. It's good and right to treat others with respect. It's important to protect the environment. Principles are excellent, but they don't have the same base.

For this same reason, Marlow, the protagonist in Joseph Conrad's *Heart of Darkness*, argues that principles won't necessarily carry one through in the midst of challenges. "Principles won't do," he says. "You want a deliberate belief." In the novel, we see Kurtz, the man Marlow is eager to meet, descend into savagery. For much of the novel, Kurtz seems like the British ideal. He's running the Inner Station, and he's producing lots of ivory; he seems to have it all together. Others in the novel demonstrate the same adherence to propriety that Kurtz seems to as well. But as we follow Marlow on his journey to the center of Africa, we learn that these principles—following rules, wearing the right clothes, doing the correct jobs—won't do. Kurtz abandons his principles when greed overtakes him.

Principles don't always hold up when challenged, and, although they may encourage good works, they don't necessitate them as faith does. Faith, or "a deliberate belief" in God, requires action. Christians do good not out of principle, but because we serve a God who is good.

> In the same way, faith by itself, if it is not accompanied by action, is dead. But someone will say, "You have faith; I have deeds." Show me your faith without deeds, and I will show you my faith by my deeds. (James 2:17–18, NIV)

Crooked Little Heart

> Rosie and Marisa rallied for the critical point, until Marisa hit a ball near the baseline. And it was not solidly on the line, but it was definitely in, touching half an inch of white. It was the most basic rule of tennis sportsmanship that you always gave your opponent the benefit of any doubt. If her ball was so close you honestly couldn't say for sure whether it was in or out, you played it in.[1]
>
> —ANNE LAMOTT, *CROOKED LITTLE HEART*

In a discussion about the fruit of the Spirit, I remember a student saying, "You know, it just occurred to me that bearing fruit implies being healthy." His comment made me think about one of the apple trees in the backyard of the house where we used to live. This tree didn't produce many apples, and the ones it did produce were certainly not something you would pick up and eat; they were puny and deformed. No doubt this was due to our lack of attention to the tree beyond admiring its white blossoms each spring.

The fruit of the Spirit includes faithfulness. What comes to your mind when you think of being faithful? Being faithful is essential to a good marriage, for example. Or, in a similar vein, God commanded the Israelites to be faithful, meaning don't worship anyone (or anything) else. To get a grasp of what faithful is, maybe we should turn to Anne Lamott's example of what *unfaithful* looks like.

In her novel *Crooked Little Heart*, Lamott gives remarkable insight into unfaithfulness. Each character in the novel has some flaw—large or small—that prevents him or her from being faithful. The main character, Rosie, has a problem with faithfulness when she plays tournament tennis. She loves the game and plays

---

1. Lamott, *Crooked Little Heart*, 85.

hard and well. But every now and then, she cheats. In one particularly revealing scene, she is playing Marisa, and the ball Marisa hits is just barely on the line. And Rosie decides, for the first time in her tennis career, to cheat:

"The ball was definitely, though barely, in, and time became thick and vacuumy and so silent that it was almost noise, and Rosie turned as if to hit this backhand, and without really thinking much about it, caught the ball and called it out. Nonchalantly, heart pounding, Rosie whacked the ball over the net to a stunned Marisa and walked to the forehand court.

'That wasn't out,' said Marisa. 'That hit the line.'

'No,' said Rosie innocently, 'it was just barely out.'"[2]

And every time Rosie resorts to this act of unfaithfulness after this critical moment, she feels just a little dirtier. But it also gets easier.

Where do we need to cultivate faithfulness in our lives? It takes courage to look at ourselves and acknowledge where we have been compromising our integrity. We need to recognize the places where our unfaithfulness has made us smaller, deformed people. If each day becomes a God-conscious journey, we will bear healthy fruit and thrive in the Spirit's garden.

> Whoever can be trusted with very little can also be trusted with much, and whoever is dishonest with very little will also be dishonest with much. (Luke 16:10, NIV)

---

2. Lamott, *Crooked Little Heart*, 86.

Tested

> "Father, I betrayed you. I trampled on the picture of Christ,"
> said Kichijiro with tears. "In this world are the strong and
> the weak. The strong never yield to torture, and they go to
> Paradise; but what about those, like myself, who are born
> weak, those who, when tortured and ordered to trample on
> the sacred image, give in?"[1]
>
> —SHŪSAKU ENDŌ, *SILENCE*

Silence is one of the most beautiful books I have ever read. It is
the story of a priest named Rodrigues who is sent from his native country of Portugal to be a missionary to the Christians in
Japan in the early 1600s. Christianity had flourished there in pre-
vious years, but at this time priests were going there to fortify the
Japanese Christians as they were being persecuted and tortured for
their faith. Throughout the novel, a very irritating character named
Kichijiro keeps showing up at the oddest times. He was supposed
to be a native Japanese Christian who could help the priests, but
over and over again he renounces his faith when he is captured so
that he can avoid torture. One of the most terrible things he does is
to turn in the priest for a few pieces of silver. The parallel to Judas
in the Bible is not lost on the reader—or on Rodrigues.

Strangely, Kichijiro keeps coming back to be forgiven. His
excuse is that he wants to be a brave martyr for his faith, but
he is just too weak. And although one is tempted to dismiss his
excuses, the fact that the torture involves being hung over a pit
upside down for a slow death makes even the priest pity him. To
prove that a prisoner has rejected Christianity, they are required
to step on an image of Christ and spit upon it. Kichiljiro does so
several times in the story. And each time, he dissolves into shame

---

1. Endō, *Silence*, 190.

and tears and begs the priest to hear his confession. The same confession each time.

I would like to say that I resonated with the character Rodrigues, who refused to deny his love for Christ even in the face of God's continuous silence, even in the face of impending torture and death. He defends his faith to his captors with eloquence and profound insight. But I cannot help fearing that I more closely resemble Kichiljiro. How would I respond to the threat of such terrible torture and the loss of those I love? There is no way of knowing, of course, but devotion and faith must be able to withstand testing to determine their validity. We do not know what we are capable of—for good or ill—until we are tested.

Put aside the dramatic nature of this story's testing. How effectively does my life offer proof for my faith on ordinary days? There are countless small ways we are tested every day, like defending unpopular convictions, or reaching out to support someone we would prefer not to associate with, or refusing to participate in small compromises of integrity and character. Or, like Rodrigues, holding on to God with all our might, even when he is silent, even when every trace of him seems to have disappeared.

The good news is that the Kichiljiros of this world are welcomed back into the embrace of God time and time again. In the words of Rodrigues: "But Christ did not die for the good and beautiful. It is easy enough to die for the good and beautiful; the hard thing is to die for the miserable and corrupt."[2]

> But we have this treasure in jars of clay to show that this all-surpassing power is from God and not from us. (2 Corinthians 4:7, NIV)

2. Endō, *Silence*, 38

Bibliography

Achebe, Chinua. *Things Fall Apart*. New York: Anchor, 1994.

Alexie, Sherman. *The Absolutely True Diary of a Part-Time Indian*. New York: Little, Brown, 2007.

Augustine. *The Confessions*. United Kingdom: Hendrickson, 2004.

Backman, Fredrik. *A Man Called Ove: A Novel*. New York: Washington Square, 2012.

Baum, L. Frank. *The Wizard of Oz*. Ware: Wordsworth Classics, 1993.

Benet, Stephen Vincent. "By the Waters of Babylon." In *Appreciating Literature*. Mission Hills, CA: Glencoe, 1991.

Crisman, Steve, dir. *Biography—Ernest Hemingway: Wrestling with Life*. Narrated by Mariel Hemingway. A&E DVD, 1996–2007.

Berry, Wendell. "Manifesto: The Mad Farmer Liberation Front." In *The Country of Marriage*. United Kingdom: Harcourt, Brace, 1974.

Bierma, Lyle D. *The Theology of the Heidelberg Catechism*. Louisville: Westminster John Knox, 2013.

"Brain Hacking." *CBS News*, April 9, 2017. https://www.cbsnews.com/video/brain-hacking/.

Bradbury, Ray. *Fahrenheit 451*. New York: Simon & Schuster, 2013.

———. "All Summer in a Day." In *Elements of Literature*, edited by G. Kylene Beers. Austin, TX: Holt, Rinehart and Winston, 2002.

Brittain, Vera. *Testament of Youth: An Autobiographical Study of the Years 1900-1925*. London: Fontana, 1979.

Brooks, David. *The Road to Character*. New York: Random House, 2015.

Buechner, Frederick. *The Hungering Dark*. New York: Harper & Row, 1969.

———. *A Room Called Remember*. New York: Harper & Row, 1984.

———. *Wishful Thinking: A Theological ABC*. New York: Harper & Row, 1973.

Burns, Robert. "To A Mouse." *Poems, Chiefly in the Scottish Dialect*. United Kingdom: M'Kie, 1786.

Card, Orson Scott. *Ender's Game*. New York: Tor, 1991.

Chiang, Ted. "Story of Your Life." In *Stories of Your Life and Others*. New York: Knopf Doubleday, 2010.

Cisneros, Sandra. *The House on Mango Street*. New York: Vintage, 1983.

Clark, Walter Van Tilburg. "The Portable Phonograph." *The Age of Anxiety: Modern American Stories*, edited by C. Jeriel Howard and Richard Francis Tracz. Boston: Allyn & Bacon, 1972.

Conrad, Joseph. *Heart of Darkness*. Mineola, NY: Dover, 2012.

Cuddy, Amy. "Your Body Language May Shape Who You Are." *TED*, June 2012. www.ted.com/talks/amy_cuddy_your_body_language_may_shape_ who_you_are?language=en.

cummings, e. e. "i thank You God for most this amazing." In *Xaipe*. New York: Liveright, 1997.

Douglass, Frederick. *Narrative of the Life of Frederick Douglass, an American Slave*. New York: Barnes and Noble, 2003.

Dunbar, Paul Laurence. *Complete Poems of Paul Laurence Dunbar: An African American Poet, Novelist and Playwright in the Late 19th Century*. Adansonia, 2018.

Edmundson, Henry T., III. *A Political Companion to Flannery O'Connor*. Lexington, KY: The University Press of Kentucky, 2017.

Edwards, Jonathan. "Sinners in the Hands of an Angry God." In *Early American Writing*, edited by Giles B. Gunn. New York: Penguin, 1994.

Eliot, T. S. "The Hollow Men." *The Complete Poems and Plays, 1909-1950*. United Kingdom: Harcourt, Brace, 1971.

Emerson, Ralph Waldo. "Nature." *Nature, Addresses, and Lectures*. Honolulu: University Press of the Pacific, 2001.

Endō, Shūsaku. *Silence*. Translated by William Johnston. N.p.: Taplinger, 1999.

Fitzgerald, F. Scott. *The Great Gatsby: The Authorized Text*. London: Scribner's, 1953.

Francis, Pope. "Twitter / @Pontifex: In confession we encounter. . ." August 12, 2016, 7:30 a.m. https://twitter.com/Pontifex/status/764061489493794816.

Frost, Robert. *The Poetry of Robert Frost: The Collected Poems*. Edited by Edward Connery. New York: Holt, 1969.

Gandhi, Arun, and Bethany Hegedus. *Be the Change: A Grandfather Gandhi Story*. New York: Atheneum, 2016.

Golding, William. *Lord of the Flies*. New York: Penguin, 2016.

Hosseini, Khaled. *The Kite Runner*. New York: Riverhead, 2003.

Hemingway, Ernest. *A Farewell to Arms*. London: Scribner's, 1957.

Henley, William E. "Invictus." In *Lyra Heroica: A Book of Verse for Boys*. Creative Media Partners, 2018.

Hugo, Victor. *The Complete Poems by Victor Hugo*. London: Delphi Classics, 2017.

Hurston, Zora Neale. *Their Eyes Were Watching God*. New York: Perennial Classics, 1998.

Huxley, Aldous. *Brave New World; and, Brave New World Revisited*. San Francisco: Harper Perennial Modern Classics, 2005.

Irving, Washington. "The Devil and Tom Walker." *The Legend of Sleepy Hollow and Other Tales, Or, The Sketchbook of Geoffrey Crayon, Gent*. New York: Modern Library, 2001.

Isaacson, Walter. "In Search of the Real Bill Gates." *Time*, January 13, 1997. http://content.time.com/time/magazine/article/0,9171,1120657,00.html.

Jackson, Shirley. "The Possibility of Evil." *Shirley Jackson's American Gothic*. Albany: State University of New York Press, 2003.

Johnson, Adam. *The Orphan Master's Son: A Novel*. New York: Random House, 2012.

Kalb, Claudia. "These Are History's Most Notorious Liars." *National Geographic*, June 2017. https://www.nationalgeographic.com/magazine/2017/06/famous -liars/.

Knowles, John. *A Separate Peace*. London: Scribner Classics, 1987.

Lamott, Anne. *Crooked Little Heart*. New York: Anchor, 1997.

Lee, Harper. *To Kill A Mockingbird*. New York: Warner, 1960.

Lewis, C. S. *The Great Divorce: A Dream*. San Francisco: Harper One, 2001.

———. *Mere Christianity*. San Francisco: HarperCollins, 2001.

———. *Out of the Silent Planet*. London: Scribner's, 1996.

———. *Perelandra*. London: Simon & Schuster, 1972.

———. *The Problem of Pain*. New York: Collier, 1962.

———. *The Screwtape Letters*. New York: Macmillan, 1961.

———. *The Weight of Glory and Other Addresses*. New York: Macmillan, 1980.

———. *Yours, Jack: Spiritual Direction from C.S. Lewis*. San Francisco: HarperCollins, 2008.

Lowry, Lois. *The Giver*. New York: Random House, 1993.

Miller, Arthur. *The Crucible*. London: Penguin, 1995.

Milton, John. "Sonnet 19." *The Oxford Book of English Verse, 1250-1900*. London: Clarendon, 1901.

Neff, David. "You Can't Think Your Way to God." *Christianity Today*, May 24, 2013. www.christianitytoday.com/ct/2013/may/you-cant-think-your-way- to-god.html.

Ng, Celeste. *Little Fires Everywhere*. London: Penguin, 2017.

O'Brien, Tim. *In the Lake of the Woods*. London: Penguin, 1995.

———. *The Things They Carried: A Work of Fiction*. New York: Broadway, 2004.

O'Connor, Flannery. *Flannery O'Connor: The Complete Stories*. Edited by Sally Fitzgerald. New York: Farrar, Straus & Giroux, 1972.

Plantinga, Cornelius. *Engaging God's World: A Christian Vision of Faith, Learning, and Living*. Grand Rapids, MI: Eerdmans, 2002.

Potok, Chaim. *The Chosen*. New York: Fawcett Crest, 1967.

Robbins, Tim, dir. *Dead Man Walking*. 1995. Gramercy Pictures. Film.

Robinson, Robert. "Come Thou Fount of Every Blessing." *Lift Up Your Hearts*. Faith Alive, 2013.

Rohr, Richard. "Utterly Humbled by Mystery." *NPR*, December 18, 2006. www. npr.org/templates/story/story.php?storyId=6631954.

Shakespeare, William. *Hamlet*. London: Simon & Schuster, 2012.

———. *Macbeth*. London: Simon & Schuster, 2004.

Shaw, Bernard. *Pygmalion*. Clayton, DE: Prestwick, 2014.

Shea, John. *The Spiritual Wisdom of the Gospels for Christian Preachers and Teachers*. Collegeville, MN: Liturgical, 2006.

Shelley, Mary. *Frankenstein, Or, The Modern Prometheus*. Signet Classics. N.p.: Perfection Learning, 2013.

Shilling, Lilless McPherson, and Linda K. Fuller, eds. *Dictionary of Quotations in Communications*. Westport, CT: Greenwood, 1997.

Spangler, Ann. *Praying the Attributes of God: A Daily Guide to Experiencing His Greatness*. Carol Stream: Tyndale, 2013.

Spiegelman, Art. *Maus II: A Survivor's Tale: And Here My Troubles Began*. New York: Pantheon, 1986.

Steinbeck, John. *The Grapes of Wrath*. New York: Penguin, 1976.

Thoreau, Henry David. *Walden*. Boston: Beacon, 1997.

Vonnegut, Kurt. *Cat's Cradle*. New York: Dial, 2010.

———. *A Man Without a Country*. United States: Seven Stories, 2011.

———. *Slaughterhouse-Five, or, The Children's Crusade: A Duty-Dance with Death*. New York: Dial, 2009.

Wesley, John. "Amazing Grace." *Lift Up Your Hearts*. Faith Alive, 2013.

Williams, William Carlos. "The Red Wheelbarrow." In *Poetry for Young People: William Carlos Williams*, edited by Christopher MacGowan and Robert Crockett, 27. New York: Sterling, 2004.

Wright, N. T. *After You Believe: Why Christian Character Matters*. United Kingdom: HarperCollins, 2010.

Wyche, Steve. "Colin Kaepernick Explains Why He Sat during National Anthem." www.nfl.com/news/colin-kaepernick-explains-why-he-sat-during -national-anthem-0ap3000000691077.

Yancey, Philip. *What's So Amazing About Grace?* Grand Rapids, Michigan: Zondervan, 1997.

A Year of Beautiful Thoughts. Compiled by Jeanie Ashley Bates Greenough, United States: Crowell, 1902.